PALE ALE

BREWDOG

PUNK IPA

POST MODERN CLASSIC

Saison
Dupont

Brasserie Dupont

RA NEVADA

E ALE

CRAFTED ALE

CRAFT
CRAFT
CRAFT BEER
FT PROP
BEER
CRAFT
CRAFT
CRAFT BEER
FT PROP

CRAFT BEER FOR THE PEOPLE

An Hachette UK Company
www.hachette.co.uk

First published in Great Britain in 2017 by Mitchell Beazley, a division of
Octopus Publishing Group Ltd
Carmelite House
50 Victoria Embankment
London EC4Y 0DZ
www.octopusbooks.co.uk
www.octopusbooksusa.co.uk

Distributed in the USA by Hachette Book Group
1290 Avenue of the Americas
4th and 5th Floors
New York, NY 10020

Distributed in Canada by Canadian Manda Group
664 Annette St, Toronto, Ontario, Canada M6S 2C8

ISBN 978-1-78472-295-1

A CIP catalogue record for this book is available from the British Library.

Printed and bound in China

10 9 8 7 6 5 4 3 2

Group publishing director Denise Bates
Senior editor Pauline Bache
Creative director (for Octopus) Jonathan Christie
Creative director (for BrewDog) Simon Shaw
Designer Jack Storey
Special photography Paul Winch-Furness and Karl Adamson
Food styling Sian Henley
Home brewer Brew Builder & mrlard (Mark Krawiec – www.brewbuilder.co.uk)
Senior production manager Katherine Hockley

All gallon measures are US gallons

CRAFT BEER FOR THE PEOPLE

Richard Taylor
with James Watt & Martin Dickie

MITCHELL
BEAZLEY

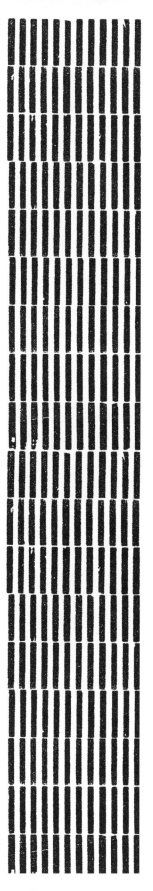

CONTENTS

INTRODUCTION

MAKING OTHER PEOPLE AS PASSIONATE ABOUT GREAT CRAFT BEER AS WE ARE

CRAFT BEER FOR THE PEOPLE

Craft beer is a force for all that is good in this world.

No, really.

This book is our opportunity to prove that to you; to tell you just how amazing craft beer is. How it embraces flavour and passion over everything else. How it fosters innovation and experimentation rather than focusing purely on the bottom line or a faceless costings spreadsheet. And how it brings people together all around the world, thanks to the hard work, persistence and dedication of those in the craft beer industry.

But we'll start right back at the beginning. Your beginning. Well, not your actual beginning (we'll leave that to other specialists), but your beery origins instead. Think back to the story of your first beer. Chances are you remember when, where and what it was. Maybe one of your parents let you taste theirs when you were little, only for your face to fold in disgust?

Or your first beer could have been more than just a mouthful. Perhaps it was a surreptitious can sneaked away and opened in a top-secret location. Or the product of that first nervous approach to a bar, fingers knuckle-white around that brand-new ID. With a rehearsed speech inwardly playing over and over, your mouth opening and the beer order spilling out in a voice higher-pitched than Elmo having his nuts slammed in a drawer.

Anyway. Three points related to the story of your first beery experience. First, it's likely that the beer these youthful indiscretions secured wasn't worth all the effort; you didn't like it, or it was a struggle to get through it. But the second point is that it didn't matter in the least. That first encounter opened your eyes.

The experience of trying your first beer is a rite of passage: the dawning of a new world. That feeling of excitement and discovery is something that stays with beer drinkers throughout their lives. Trying new things is the cornerstone of what craft beer is about (from a socially acceptable hour onward), and it all begins with that initial moment of exploration. It stays with you.

The third point of note is that all these tales of first encounters of the beery kind relate to that particular beverage. We'd wager that there are far fewer heroic tales of that earliest glass of wine, or memorable forays into the joys of the Jägerbomb. Chances are it was beer that whetted your drinking whistle. And there is a very important reason that underpins this.

Beer is of and for the people.

No other drink has done more to bring people together and give them a common bond around which to rally. No, not even tea. Beer has fostered relationships, partnerships and companionship for centuries. Ever since the days of hieroglyphs and three-sided buildings, it is to beer that people have turned at the end of the day or the start of the weekend. Beer is mankind's greatest social lubricant.

BEER IS OF AND FOR THE PEOPLE.

It is not elitist or out of touch – quite the opposite. It cuts through the social divide to be enjoyed by everyone. The great houses of antiquity needed beer in order to keep functioning. European fields would have remained unharvested without it. Armies marched to the sound of beer bottles. Even US presidents brewed their own.

Beer is immediate, on target and there when you need it. It is the perfect refresher, disappearing within moments of touching the glass, yet also the ideal fireside companion to nurse into the small hours. Beer can be enjoyed in any location, at any time of year, in any weather (we brew in northeastern Scotland. Take it from us).

It tastes just as good by an iridescent shoreline on a blazing summer's afternoon as it does within the comforting embrace of a centuries-old pub in a small village whose name you can't pronounce. Its diversity and range are dizzying and very nearly endless, as more innovations appear from breweries every day of the week. This is beer's greatest secret: its variety. And this is down to the sheer number of different styles that exist.

From clean, crisp Pilsners and golden ales that leave herbal and floral notes on your palate, to thunderous imperial stouts and barrel-aged beers you can taste after you brush your teeth, beer has a range like no other. Craft brewers are riffing on traditional styles by introducing an array of ingredients and processes that showcase every step of the flavour spectrum.

And that's another reason why beer is awesome (we've lost count how many there have been so far). None of this is static. There can be no status quo when the ground rules are shifting with each addition of grain to a mash tun, each

filling of a whisky cask with beer. Craft beer doesn't hide behind outdated methods or a quirk of geography. The only rule that matters is that you should brew the best beer you can in the best way possible.

Because in the end, the people decide. The recent boom in craft beer over mass-produced; independent breweries over controlled; and flavour over insipidness has been driven by a single, all-encompassing factor: public demand. You guys are more interested in locally produced, high-quality craft beer than ever before.

And that's where this book comes in.

Craft Beer for the People is this entire attitude brought to life – a beer book to instil the same passion and belief in the amazing world of beer that we bring to work every day here at BrewDog. In this book we will take you from the genesis of the craft beer revolution and show you the very basics of how to taste beer as a fully sensory experience. The Physics uncovers the mystery of how four humble ingredients pull together into this wonderful drink and shows the best way to store your beers to ensure you enjoy the brewer's best. Craft on Deck will take you on a journey through the myriad and wonderful styles of beers, from the most common gateway brew, lager, through to today's trendy and innovative wild cards. DIY Dog allows you to embrace the role of brewer for yourself, either brewing with stabilizers for your first extract brew, or going the whole shebang and brewing from scratch. For inspiration, we have included recipes for our most iconic beers and ten from the craft breweries we most admire (many published for the first time). Finally, Dog Eat Dog gives a new opportunity to enjoy beer either alongside or within fantastic recipes for beer lovers. All along the way we'll feature brew sheets on our top beers, drop ticks for you to blot onto the page every time you try a new brew, and spotter's guides for you to use when you're out enjoying a couple with your friends.

That's because this book is to be learned from, have notes added to, spilled on. This is a journal, not a coffee-table deadweight; a window into our world and a repository of information. Take it to heart and take it to bars.

After all, the first beer you tried resulted in a unique and individual moment – this book is your chance to continue your beery adventures in the same vein.

We can all drink to that.

ENJOYING BEER

01

WHAT IS CRAFT BEER?

To paraphrase Oscar Wilde, craft beer is the unstoppable pursuit of the indefinable.

This modern term that screams out from bar chalkboards and bottle labels the length of the country must mean something. At first it brings to mind rustic workshops with sawdust hanging in beams of afternoon sunlight, or craft stalls with tables bearing hand-stitched cushions and earrings made from seashells. Isn't beer just…well, beer?

Let's start with an analogy.

Imagine, for a minute, that music is your overriding passion. Entranced by that first Nirvana/ Miles Davis/Ace of Base track you heard, you were drawn in. From that moment, you wanted to make music at the expense of everything else. So at home you picked up a guitar or a pair of drumsticks, or began writing lyrics.

And the results were terrible. You couldn't hit any notes; your voice fumbled rather than soared. But instead of quitting you kept going. You were bad, but f**k it – you just did it anyway. And after months or even years of practice at home, you reached a level of skill and confidence where you could audition to join a band.

So you did.

At first your band also struggled – using new equipment, working together instead of individually made things hard. It took a while to get everything and everyone in sync. But you kept on, driven by your all-consuming love of music.

Eventually you started to play gigs, even though nobody knew who you were. Only your parents and close friends showed up – and they only said the right things when you asked for feedback. But one day people you didn't know paid money to discover what you were about.

This was the moment you had dreamed of ever since you started out playing at home, alone. Yet the hard work still continued, with long hours and relatively little reward at the end of each day. It took months or even years of effort, until you began to notice a difference.

Eventually, after your band had logged dozens of new releases and attended more festivals than you could hope to remember, word of mouth had spread to the extent where people were handing over enough money for you and your bandmates to begin to earn a modest living.

You had finally made it.

And then almost overnight, there was a new band everyone was talking about on the TV. They looked the part, but to you there was something not quite right about them. When they played their instruments, they were actually miming. They were all swagger; no substance.

Genuine music fans could spot the difference a mile off, but people new to the genre flocked to their music. Even when it turned out that this new band had been put together by a record label, styled to look and sound like they belonged. All your hard work, long hours and knockbacks were bypassed in days.

The big money men had arrived and they had brought their impostors with them. Your style of music had become so successful, they were attempting to commoditize it. While you were in it for the love of music, they were only interested in the bottom line. Your spirit of creativity and adventure had been piggybacked on overnight.

How would this make you feel?

The craft beer movement is gaining a greater share of the market with each passing year through the passion and skill of those who wield brewing equipment (as opposed to instruments). From careers honed through homebrewing to collaborations between like-minded breweries around the world, it is a movement driven by creativity.

When any creative industry breaks into the mainstream, others take notice. Just as with big record labels and their manufactured acts, the money men in brewing have cottoned on to the success and hard work of others. They want a slice of craft beer.

Typically, there are two ways they go about this. Industrial lager brands are now creating fake craft beer that looks authentic, but on closer inspection mimes the instruments. This so-called "crafty" beer is an affront to everyone who worked hard to get where they are.

The other tactic to which corporate beer resorts is even more abrupt; they simply take over existing craft breweries. It's ambulance-chasing on a grand scale – see who is doing well and adopt chequebook diplomacy. Screw the people who work for the breweries and buy the name.

It may be oafish, but why is it a problem?

Well, for those of us truly passionate about the craft beer sector, these newcomers devalue the term, as they seek to confuse and hoodwink the beer drinker. The beers are like band T-shirts worn by people who can't name an album and the companies are simply snake-oil salesmen.

Everything we and many other craft breweries up and down the country work for is done for the love of brewing amazing beer, using the best ingredients, in the right way. Craft beer is a point of difference. A rallying call and a badge of recognition: not something these newcomers should be able to hide behind.

But this is where you come in.

CRAFT BEER IS FOR THE PEOPLE. PURVEYORS OF SNAKE OIL NEED NOT APPLY.

Whether you're a beer veteran or a virgin, read up a little. Such is the variety of amazing beer out there, research rewards in kind. Visit your local craft brewer. Follow them on social media (craft brewers usually handle their own rather than paying a branding agency). Try as many different styles as you can; listen to recommendations.

So when faced with a new "craft beer" from a "craft brewery" that you haven't seen before, you can be your own best judge. Sample it against something similar you know and trust. It won't take more than a few sips of each to learn what flashy advertising, big budgets and profiling can't hide.

MEETING THE BEER HUNTER

"IF THIS IS WHAT YOU CAN DO THEN I SUGGEST YOU LEAVE YOUR JOBS IMMEDIATELY AND OPEN A BREWERY."

In our early days, we were ready to put everything on the line to pursue our dream of opening a brewery, and we knew what a colossal undertaking running our own business would be. But it was advice from someone we didn't know that helped us over the line.

Michael Jackson was a pioneer in the world of beer appreciation and writing, and his "Beer Hunter" articles and lectures inspired a generation of people to believe that beer was a quality product to rival any other. In his own words, his intention was "to elevate the understanding, the diversity and the nobility of beer".

Through his books and television programmes, he enlightened those who thought of beer as a singular entity – whatever they served at your local pub or bar – and introduced different styles and brewing regions of the world, distinctive ingredients and the passion of brewers. He put beer on the map, pure and simple. Then, it was totally (instead of mostly) overshadowed by wine in the media. Michael hauled it into public consciousness. We were similarly passionate about beer – and in 2007, when an opportunity to meet him arose, we knew we had to.

Michael was as convivial a man as you could hope to meet, but we decided to introduce ourselves and then let our beer do the rest of the talking. We had brought two beers for him to try, and poured both of them for him to give his honest appraisal.

So it came to pass that beers created in Martin's garage were in the glass of a man who had done more than any other to make the country aware of the awesome variety and range of beers that were out there. We gave him Rip Tide and Paradox, which had been aged in a single Islay whisky cask, and nervously awaited the verdict.

"Boys," he said, looking over his glasses, "if this is what you can do, then I suggest you leave your jobs immediately and open a brewery."

This justification – and relief – was incredible. The Beer Hunter himself loved our garage-brewed beer and confirmed what we were thinking. It was the moment we realized we could – and more importantly, should – make a go of it. His encouragement was all we needed. At this meeting, BrewDog was born.

GATEWAY BEER

Do you remember the first beer you tried? Do you remember the first good beer you tried? Chances are they were very different, and drunk under totally dissimilar circumstances (and likely with differing outcomes as well). Just as very few people experiment with smoking by trying Cuban cigars or cooking for themselves by rustling up a lobster thermidor, that first beer was probably something quite other than a freshly served craft beer in a branded glass. But you know what? That's OK. It's why we have gateway beers – lightbulb moments in liquid form.

Not all beer drinkers have a gateway – some just charge in and enjoy whatever they can get their hands on – but for many of us, the transition from industrial lager to a beer that actually tastes of something is done via the medium of one specific game-changer. These beers can appear in the hands of the previously unenlightened in one of several ways: via a recommendation from a friend, perhaps, or a random punt from a colourful shelf, or a sudden unexplained desire to find out what everyone else is discussing on your nights out drinking.

The mechanisms for acquiring a gateway beer are varied, but the result is the same; it's not why you came to taste that particular beer that matters, but what it does to your tastebuds immediately following that first sip: that chain reaction going off in your head, lighting a fuse that can never be snuffed out. The moment you open and go through that gateway, there's no going back. Whether finally appeasing your friend (or partner) and trying that beer, or simply drinking one because it had nothing more than an interesting label, beer will never be the same again.

But what exactly do we mean by a gateway beer?

Well, we can best illustrate the concept with an example, one of the most storied of all in the entire genre – Sierra Nevada Pale Ale. This is a beer that is not only a gateway, but a true pioneer. First brewed in November 1980, it has inspired countless brewers over the intervening decades (not least ourselves). A stone-cold classic, it was one of the first beers to use the Cascade hop and has remained at the top of the craft brewing tree for over 30 years. As such, there is no better introduction to the wonders of the art Sierra Nevada themselves helped forge.

Their industry-defining pale ale is the ideal gateway beer because it fulfils the all-important "three As"...

ACCESSIBILITY

Anybody who arrives into the world of beer from the standing start of base lager has only a single direction in which they can travel; Sierra Nevada Pale Ale isn't just a step up, it's a hop-charged, skyscraper-clearing leap. And yet, it's not punishing. There's no tongue-withering bitterness or strange aftertaste – it is a pure citrus medley held together with a fantastic balance. It has a grassy, floral aroma and a winningly refreshing finish. If anybody is wary of craft beer because of the outlandish reputation it has, give them this.

AVAILABILITY

The beer that inspires some people to turn their backs on mass-produced, lowest-common-denominator brewing may well be something obscure and available only in a single taproom that opens on a Wednesday lunchtime in April – but true gateway beers are readily accessible to all. Sierra Nevada Pale Ale is sold in most large-scale supermarkets and in any liquor store worth its salt, so is a much more likely prospect for somebody to stumble across. To bring craft beer to the people, you need a vehicle many of them can get on board, after all, like…a bus. Or a train. Something to carry enough people to wherever that metaphor was supposed to go, anyway.

APPROACHABILITY

It may be an oft-overlooked facet of the beer world, but the best entry-level bottles – the ones that capture people's attention – are the ones that stand out. They have to look appealing, with flavour descriptors on the label so that potential customers know what they are getting. Some decry this flowery tasting language, but it worked for wine and got people to relate to a drink they previously didn't get – and that is exactly the idea with gateway beers. Plus, to flip things around, there's a reason many modern wines have colourful, wacky labels – they are aping craft beer and the success our industry has had with shaking up an old scene and appealing to new audiences.

As you are reading this book, then you may have already passed through the gate – or maybe this is the final piece of encouragement *DO IT* you need to try a beer you've not had before. But for those others following along in our wake, there are dangers lurking in the waters. You see, this concept of gateway beer is a powerful one – once somebody wakes up, they can stick with their new best beer for some time (which there is nothing wrong with). The issue is that breweries that manufacture industrial beers know this too. And they are now creating beers to entrap the unwary – gateways that lead nowhere.

As we said before, these sometimes-called "crafty" beers look like the real thing – but they are not. If you looked through our description of what craft beer is and thought,

THERE IS SO MUCH VARIETY OUT THERE, IF YOU KEEP TRYING TO GET THROUGH, EVENTUALLY ONE OF THESE GATES WILL OPEN.

"What does it matter?", then the answer lies with beers like these. The sole reason for their existence is to keep the craft-curious enmeshed in a world run by balance sheets and corporations, rather than by ingredients, ingenuity and passion. Picture the scene: a potential craft beer convert tries one of the impostor beers, after hearing about craft beer from his or her friends. The first taste is supposed to be an amazing life-changing experience. Get ready tastebuds! Time to be blown away!

And, meh.

Well, it's alright. Not that exciting really. Not sure what all the fuss was about. "Do you want another craft beer?" No, that's OK. I'll stick to my light lager, thanks. And that person will never know what they could have enjoyed. Sure, we're being slightly dramatic, but there is a serious point here. These beers are fakes hanging next to originals, simply there to trick people.

Anyway, for examples of genuine gateway beers that will lead you onto the amazing, varied world of beer brewed for the right reasons, check out the guide to beer styles starting on page 84. As you are now aware if you weren't already, there is a lot of choice out there; no shortage of beers to sample. That can be an issue as well: the near-unlimited choice of styles, flavours and added ingredients produced by tens of thousands of breweries around the world – there's just so much out there to bamboozle people looking for a gateway. But of course, that is all part of the fun.

Not everybody has a gateway beer, as we said at the start – some people leap the fence instead and get stuck in. But for every person who finds themselves thinking anew about beer after a single glass of something amazing, there are many others who repeatedly try these so-called gateways and just don't like them. That's fine – in fact, it's kind of the point. Not every gate opens if you rattle it. But the beauty of craft beer is there is so much variety out there, if you keep trying to get through, eventually one of these gates will open.

And once you have gone through it, leave it open for others (this is not a real-life farm gate; we are still in metaphor-land). If someone you know asks you about beer, use it as an example. If they are looking for something more interesting than what they are drinking at the moment, pay it forward. After all, your gateway might be exactly the same one that somebody else has been trying to find for years. Help them through it and enjoy your new life of amazing flavours – whichever gate you went through.

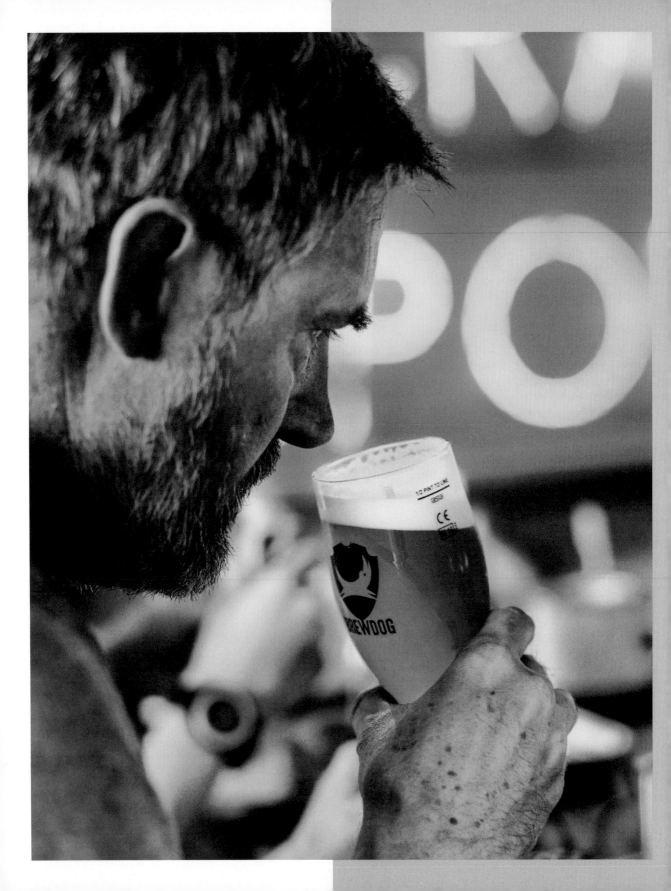

HOW TO TASTE BEER

All right, we know it's pretty straightforward. Find a bottle opener, or negotiate your way back from the bar without face planting, and all you need do is raise your glass and remember to open your mouth in time. But brewers don't work their socks off, bar staff don't put in the long hours, and those who grow and harvest barley, wheat and hops don't go out in all weathers just so the beer their efforts culminate in can be thrown back without a second thought. How you drink beer is up to you, but this is the good stuff we are talking about – at the very least, it deserves attention; it deserves to be appreciated rather than shotgunned. So how do you go about that?

Well, there are two fantastic things on your side. First, despite the vast numbers of different beer types that are out there (see the entirety of "Craft on Deck" for further details), each and every single one of them can be appreciated using the same metrics. If you can learn how to smell, taste and appreciate one, you can do it with any other beer you can get hold of. And the second plus point is that tasting beer is entirely subjective. Everyone's palate is different, so there are no wrong answers. If someone next to you loudly proclaims their beer tastes of pineapple shavings and you can only think "Eh?", then it doesn't mean they are right and you are wrong.

The best way to begin a lifetime's appreciation of beer is to go out there and start sampling it. Make notes of what you think the beers taste of. If you drink something that does taste of pineapple, that's a flavour descriptor. Learning to appreciate beer is at its simplest learning to recognize some of these tastes in what you are drinking, and applying that knowledge to future beers. That way you build up an internal (or external – writing them down is great practice) database of "what tastes like what", which you can apply to specific beers, styles, hops or other ingredients.

We can break it down further by assessing each characteristic of a beer. And let's begin with one sense that never comes into direct contact with beer (unless you really do forget to open your mouth): what you see.

1	5	10	15	20	30	40
Very Pale Straw	Gold	Amber	Deep Amber	Brown	Deep Brown	Black

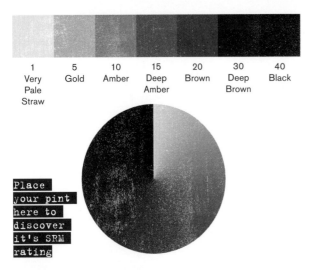

Place your pint here to discover it's SRM rating

APPEARANCE

From pin-bright lagers to imperial porters as dark as the heart of your first headmaster, beer has it all. No other beverage has such a range of colour. Several scales are designed to quantify this: degrees Lovibond, European Brewery Convention (EBC) and Standard Reference Method (SRM). The latter two are European and American stalwarts, and (of course) give slightly different readings – but the SRM scale is fairly simple to use when trying to work out what you are looking at. So here's a handy guide!

Aside from the pretty colours, the other thing to keep in mind when you're assessing a beer is how clear it is. Craft beer can arrive into your glass anything from brilliantly crystal to impenetrable (and we mean light-coloured beers – clarity is different to "darkness"). So can you pick out a slight haze? Or is the beer murky? This can be down to brewers deciding to "fine" the beer or not, removing or leaving the natural yeast behind. Or it could depend on style (lagers are usually sparklingly clear, whereas wheat beers, for instance, are often nearly opaque).

Look at what's on top as well. The size, shape and retention of the foamy head is often an indication of the quality of your beer, and how well it has been kept and served. Again this varies according to style. Wheat beers are traditionally handed over with a voluminous head, but however much is on the roof, check how it sticks to the glass as you drink: the "lacing" of concentric rings of foam that adhere to the sides as you go is another indication that the beer has been given to you in good condition.

AROMA

This is the next thing to make a note of, as the aromas are best once the beer has been fully agitated during the pour from bottle, can or bar tap. If, however, your glass is half-empty (beer glasses are never half-full), then cup your hand over the top and carefully swirl around before uncapping and taking in the aromas. This disturbance will help rouse the smells upward, and also re-invigorate the head. Get your nose in – not too far, although everyone who has ever tried to look professional and critique a beer has ended up with a frothy nose at some point. It's a badge of honour.

So, what do you smell?

Lots, probably. One way to break it down and minimize confusion is to split what you might be smelling into four parts, based on the ingredients used in the beer. So, the hops. Are they citrusy, grassy or floral? Can you smell pine resin, tree sap? Does it smell like red fruits, or something different? The Japanese hop Sorachi Ace, for example, makes some people pick out an aroma of coconut. And the malt – do you get anything like biscuits, toast, chocolate (milk or dark), roasty coffee beans or all of the above? Your beer may have some, all or none in the glass.

Next, the powerhouse – yeast. As we will learn, this can have a massive influence on the beer aroma, so how does it come over? Is it fruity? Sulphury? Does it remind you of an old blanket? A stable? It sounds strange, but quantifying these aromas by reimagining places you've been and other smells can really help.

And finally, the last of the four. We don't mean water, this time. It's any extra ingredients. If it's a cherry beer, for example, you should be able to smell cherries!

IBU

5 IBU
Mass produced lager

20 IBU
Brown Ale

35 IBU
German Pils

40+ IBU
IPA

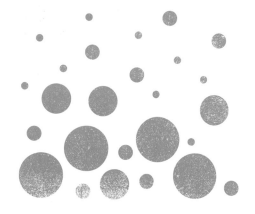

FLAVOUR

Now you can get to work. Quantifying the appearance and aroma of a beer is all well and good, but it is made to be drunk, after all – so have a sip. The retronasal passage that connects the back of your mouth upward to your nasal cavity has thousands of receptors for perceiving flavours – and this is often the reason given for beer experts saying you should swallow your beer to fully appreciate the experience (as opposed to swirling it in your mouth and spitting, like wine tasting). True – but they also say that to sound cooler than wine guys.

Once you've swallowed, take a moment to think of what you are getting – in much the same way as with the aroma. Can you taste citrus? Toffee? Banana? Mentally tag what your taste buds are going through. After a while you will be able to place these flavours much more accurately and quickly. You can help this (and your retronasal passage) by holding your breath as you swallow, then exhaling through your nose instead of your mouth. This helps stimulate all of the extra receptors and gives a fuller picture of what is going on in the beer. Just practise at home first.

The sensation in your mouth might last for quite a while – the aftertaste has a few components, but one of the most evident is bitterness. As with colour, there's a scale to measure this – the International Bitterness Units (IBU). Beers are calculated on their parts per million of dissolved alpha acids – the higher the IBU, the more bitter your beer is. Your average mass-produced lager? 5 IBU. German Pils? 35 IBU. India Pale Ales? Anything from 40 to 100, depending on how many hops are used in the brew.

MOUTHFEEL

Then you have the overall experience of drinking the beer – not the fact that it tastes of lychees or charcoal, but what other sensations you pick up. Aside from bitterness, there's the body. Is the beer watery and insipid? Or does it coat the back of your throat like cough medicine? This is dependent on the proteins remaining in the beer, with many factors involved (what malts were used, the temperature of the boil and the fermentation stage, how active the yeast was) – and it is critical to whether you enjoy it or not.

There's carbonation, as well. The amount of dissolved carbon dioxide in your beer will control this – does it effervesce over your tongue like a sparkling wine or cola? Or does it sit there, with little pop and fizz? Carbonation is down to a huge number of different factors, not least how your beer is served to you (kegged beer will have more, cask ale less) and the style of the brew you are enjoying. As a sweeping generalization, Belgian beers are more carbonated than beers from other countries. Carbonation is a horses-for-courses quality in beer appreciation!

Finally, we have the characteristic that can lead to so many wasted mornings: how strong a beer is. Measured as a percentage of ethyl alcohol by volume of beer (ABV), this factor is easily quantified by the brewers; they are required to do this, by law. Beers typically vary from 3% for milds (although beers down to 0.5% ABV exist – see page 98) up through to 4–5% for your average British pub fayre, to the modern boundary-pushing beers at 6–9% and above. And you can go above that, take it from us.

PUNK IPA

POSTMODERN CLASSIC

It all began with Punk. The first ever BrewDog beer, repeated and repeated and repeated until we had finally dialled it in to be similar to the beers that inspired us – those hoppy pale ales of the United States. Back then there was no master plan, merely a single goal: never to have to search in vain for something that we wanted to drink, ever again.

If you can't find it, make it yourself.

That was our ethos. Home-brewing became our punk rock – if the scene doesn't cater for you, start your own – and this was the result, a beer that reflected our influences and frustrations. Bitter, spiky and aggressive; a contemporary Scottish IPA, born of transatlantic fusion: North American and New Zealand hops, British malt, Scottish attitude.

Punk IPA is now our flagship beer. It is the most popular beer we brew and yet is more than just a focal point; it is a metaphor for the development of BrewDog as a whole. Start doing something you love, and it becomes more than a job. If people

like what you do, it becomes a movement. And then, most importantly of all, keep re-evaluating as you go on. Satisfaction leads to complacency.

Back in 2011, even though Punk IPA was forging ahead and had become the best-selling IPA in Scandinavia, we changed it up. We realized that the benefits of dry-hopping would let even more of the flavours and aromas spill out every time a bottle was uncapped or a beer tap flipped open. This is a lesson we learned quickly – never be afraid to revisit and reassess what you are most comfortable with.

The result was a beer that has continued to lead from the front, and a beer we believe in, every day we come to work. Our tribute to the classic IPAs of yesteryear, given a postmodern twist. Punk IPA is assertive and resinous, with tropical fruit and citrus flavour in abundance. It explodes with flavour. It is BrewDog in microcosm.

like that?
try these:

STONE IPA

6.9%

Stone Brewing, USA

Zesty, fruity and resinous –
a modern masterpiece

CANNONBALL

7.4%

Magic Rock Brewing,
England

Tropical fruit and resinous
pine in abundance from
Yorkshire's finest

THE KERNEL IPA

ABV Varies

The Kernel, England

No brewery makes better
single hop IPAs than The
Kernel

HOPPED UP IPA

RELEASED	2007
ABV	5.6%
STYLE	INDIA PALE ALE
IBU	35
HOPS	CHINOOK, SIMCOE, AHTANUM, NELSON SAUVIN, AMARILLO, CASCADE
MALT	EXTRA PALE, CARA

"PUNK IPA BEGAN WITH US BREWING
A BEER WE WANTED TO DRINK AND
ENDED UP STARTING A REVOLUTION. IT
IS OUR FLAGSHIP — ASSERTIVE, BITTER
AND WITH AN EXPLOSION OF TROPICAL
FRUIT." — JAMES WATT

"PUNK IPA WAS MY MESSIAH. IT
DELIVERED ME FROM THE EVIL OF
BLAND, TASTELESS, MASS-PRODUCED
BIG BEER AND INTO THE WELCOMING
ARMS OF THE WORLD'S CRAFT
BREWERIES." — EQUITY PUNK MATT SHAW

DROPTICK
TICK THIS BEER
OFF YOUR LIST
WITH A DROP
FROM YOUR FINGER

YOU SAY:

....
....
....
....
....
....
....
....

A DECADE OF DOG

2006

The UK beer scene was a very different place a decade ago; if you found a bar with a dozen taps it would likely sell a dozen lagers. It was a time of frustration for those seeking an alternative. Sick of the lack of decent options to drink, we made our own, armed with nothing more than some home-brew kit in Martin's garage and a desire to emulate Sierra Nevada Pale Ale. Two guys and a dog – this was how BrewDog came screaming into the world.

TWO GUYS AND A DOG – THIS WAS HOW BREWDOG CAME SCREAMING INTO THE WORLD.

2007

EMPLOYEES

2 (+1 DOG)

BEER BREWED

1,050 HL

SHARE HOLDERS

2

BREWDOG BARS

0

That chance meeting with Michael Jackson changed everything. We took £20,000 of our savings and a £30,000 bank loan (secured at the second attempt) and used it to underpin our mission to make other people as passionate about great craft beer as we were. That 50 grand equipped a dystopian lock-up in Fraserburgh in the far northeast of Scotland with enough kit to brew commercially. We learned the hard way, sleeping on sacks of malt as we went.

Every piece of advice went in one ear and out the other – brew with fewer hops, lower your prices, change the packaging. If we were going to fail, we were going to fail on our own terms. We entered a Tesco beer competition and came first, second, third and fourth – at this stage we were both living with our parents – and the overwhelming need to fulfil the new orders led to the arrival of our first employee, right at the start of 2008.

2008

EMPLOYEES

9 (+1 DOG)

BEER BREWED

4,050 HL

SHARE HOLDERS

2

BREWDOG BARS

0

Stewart Bowman joined as our second brewer, and our emphasis changed. We still wanted to brew the beers we wanted to drink (or, in Stewart's case, barrel-age), but our target had widened. We realized we had to challenge the perceptions of beer drinkers in the UK, and start a discussion. So we produced Tokyo, a 12% ABV imperial stout. These days nobody would bat an eyelid at this – but in 2008 it was deemed irresponsible, and banned.

So we increased its strength to 18.2%, and released it as Tokyo* – at the time, the strongest beer ever created in the UK. (If you're wondering about the star, it's simply to differentiate the new version from the 12% batch.) Just for good measure we also brewed a 0.5% beer to highlight the ridiculous nature of us being blamed for Britain's binge-drinking culture, and named it Nanny State. We hired more people to our fledgling crew, and doubled down on our desire to make people reconsider what beer could (and should) be about.

2009

EMPLOYEES

24 (+1 DOG)

BEER BREWED

9,500 HL

SHARE HOLDERS

1,329

BREWDOG BARS

0

But we couldn't do that by ourselves. We needed a community, an army of like-minded men and women obsessed with the variety of flavours that existed in the world of beer. So we took a huge gamble and launched our ground-breaking shareholding offering, Equity for Punks. This was our grand plan to shorten the distance between ourselves and the people who bought our beer; to give them a chance to own a part of our company.

The problem was, we'd never crowd-funded before. The first six lawyers we approached to work out the fine detail all said no, it couldn't be done. The seventh, grudgingly, said it could work. And they were right – over 1,300 people became our first wave of Equity Punks, and our anti-business business model was born. To celebrate, we brewed a 32% ABV beer, added new tanks to our brewhouse and became the UK's fastest-growing craft brewery.

2010

EMPLOYEES

39 (+1 DOG)

BEER BREWED

15,800 HL

SHARE HOLDERS

1,329

BREWDOG BARS

1

This was the year we addressed another of our concerns, born of selfishness – the fact that we couldn't find any great beers in our home city of Aberdeen. The answer was staring us in the face all along – open our own bar. It was a dream come true to be able to showcase our beers to the people of our city in the way we intended. No middlemen. A direct line of beery communication to our fans. BrewDog Aberdeen was born.

This was also the year we let experimentation take us to the boundaries of what a beer is, fusing the seldom-colliding worlds of craft beer, art and taxidermy with the 55% ABV End of History, packaged inside stuffed roadkill. We also wanted to say a personal thank you to those who had invested in our (and now their) brewery, so we hosted a cosy gathering of our Equity Punks at the first ever #PunkAGM in Aberdeen. In December 2010. The snowy one.

2011

EMPLOYEES

67 (+1 DOG)

BEER BREWED

26,750 HL

SHARE HOLDERS

6,567

BREWDOG BARS

4

BrewDog Aberdeen was going better than any of us could possibly have imagined, so when a dilapidated karaoke bar in the centre of Edinburgh became free we pulled the trigger. BrewDog Edinburgh was followed by BrewDog Glasgow and we then invaded England for our first bar south of the border, as baptized by the sight of us driving a tank down Camden High Street in London.

There to witness that opening were the second wave of BrewDog shareholders, after the launch of Equity for Punks II advanced our innovative business model and grew our community of beer-loving rebels even more. We returned to the theme of taxidermy with a beer dispensed from a deer's head – and we also went overboard with Sunk Punk, the first beer to be conditioned at the bottom of the North Sea.

2012

EMPLOYEES

135 (+1 DOG)

BEER BREWED

36,500 HL

SHARE HOLDERS

6,567

BREWDOG BARS

10

All of this we had so far achieved from a storm-weathered building on the outskirts of Fraserburgh. We had hammered the hell out of our brewkit; there was nothing more to be done. To keep up with demand we opened a state-of-the-art eco-friendly brewhouse in Ellon, 30km (20 miles) to the south. Moving was sad, but it meant we could continue to make the best beers possible (and host 2,000 Equity Punks for our second AGM).

With our new brewery up and running, beer quality became our unswerving passion. Our purpose-built brewhouse operated at maximum capacity from day one, and has never slowed. We also opened more bars in 2012, focusing on educating our customers about how amazing beer could be – which ruffled the feathers of industrial brewery giants Diageo, who prevented our bar teams from picking up an industry award we had deservedly won. #AndTheWinnerIsNot.

2013

EMPLOYEES

224 (+1 DOG)

BEER BREWED

53,500 HL

SHARE HOLDERS

14,208

BREWDOG BARS

13

The official opening of Ellon was performed not by a faceless dignitary but by one of our shareholders. Equity for Punks III welcomed over 10,000 new investors from 22 different countries, proving our message about craft beer going global. We also created the TV series *Brew Dogs*, which saw us brew with legendary beer makers from across the USA (following months of arguing that our voices didn't need subtitling for US viewers).

As well as smashing crowd-funding records, we broke through into another overseas market by opening our first International BrewDog Bar, in Stockholm, Sweden. Few countries have taken us to heart quite like Sweden; Punk IPA had been the top-selling IPA in Scandinavia for four years by this time. We had to double the size of our Ellon brewery to keep up, later that year. Oh, and we launched our ruthless IPA Jack Hammer in 2013, too.

2014

EMPLOYEES

358 (+1 DOG)

BEER BREWED

90,000 HL

SHARE HOLDERS

14,568

BREWDOG BARS

26

We had been having so much fun opening new bars around the world that we went hell for leather in 2014, flinging back the doors of a dozen new temples of craft beer in parts of the globe as eclectic as Cardiff, Tokyo, Clapham Junction and São Paulo. Our bars rock the front lines of our mission to spread the gospel of craft beer, and have become second homes for hop-heads and beer fans in all corners of the world.

Speaking of our global quest, we shipped beer to 55 different countries and recorded a second series of *Brew Dogs*. We also picked a fight with the President of Russia, releasing a beer to highlight twistedly homophobic legislation passed in the country; Hello My Name is Vladimir was brewed with "performance-enhancing" limonnik berries. To give the man himself a helping hand, we sent a case to the Kremlin. We didn't hear back.

2015

EMPLOYEES

540 (+1 DOG)

BEER BREWED

134,000 HL

SHARE HOLDERS

32,000

BREWDOG BARS

44

In 2015 we launched the largest equity crowd-funding scheme in history, Equity for Punks IV, raising the ranks of our shareholders to 32,000. To celebrate, we parachuted stuffed cats over the fat cats in the City of London – our business model puts the people who drink our beer in control, not them. To underline this, we welcomed 6,000 Equity Punks to Aberdeen for our raucous #PunkAGM.

It was also the year of aluminium as we installed a colossal canning line in our Ellon brewery and near-immediately turned it toward the production of canned Jack Hammer. We then maxed everything out with Black Eyed King Imp, at 12.7% ABV the strongest ale ever placed in a can. It was quite a year for BrewDog beer, as we released 65 different beers into the wild. Oh, and we started to reclaim a wild corner of Ohio, too…

2016

EMPLOYEES

750 (+1 DOG)

BEER BREWED

214,000 HL

SHARE HOLDERS

55,000

BREWDOG BARS

50

Such is the pace at which we move that our Ellon brewery – opened only three years previously – was upgraded in a major way with a 300hl brewhouse that increased our capacity fivefold. And that wasn't the only brewery we built in 2016 – we also broke with convention and became the first UK craft brewery to open a production brewery in America, the land that had inspired us to start homebrewing ten years earlier.

The 9,290 square metre (100,000 square feet) facility that is BrewDog Columbus was built with a single intention: to get our beer into the hands of craft beer fans in North America faster, fresher and with more flavour. If that broke convention, we then destroyed it with DIY Dog as we gave away the detailed recipes to every single BrewDog beer ever made (all 215 of them), for free, hopefully to inspire the next generation of home-brewers to have a go and kick-start their passion.

2017...

The future holds…what, for BrewDog? Increased capacity, that's a given. More innovation in every part of our business. The involvement of our epic community of shareholders in everything that we do: of course. The truth is, aside from these, we don't really know. What we will do is carry on growing as fast as we can, brewing amazing beer and adding to our unbelievable team of people around the world. We'll see where it takes us.

The year 2017 marks a "decade of dog" – ten years since we unfurled the shutters of our Fraserburgh brewery and drove the first batch of Punk IPA to the retailers in our beat-up van. So how are we going to mark this milestone? Well, by continuing what we started. By not slowing down. By making the best beer you can buy, anywhere. And by making others as passionate about craft beer as we are. To be honest, this is just the beginning…

THE PHYSICS

02

HOW IS BEER MADE?

So we've established that beer is A Wonderful Thing. The next question on the flipchart is how you go about making it. The craft beer spectrum contains a mighty array of differing styles, from fruity and floral Belgian saisons to deeply roasty imperial stouts and porters, with many more besides. These beers owe their individuality to their wide range of ingredients, and yet at the heart of brewing lies a series of steps used by every brewer. He or she will use their skill and experience to work through this process and get the raw ingredients to truly sing together as a final, finished (and then enjoyed) beer.

A useful analogy to explain this is to see brewers as chefs (although brewers tend to swear more). Those modern superheroes of the kitchen use different ingredients to create a recipe, and then use certain techniques to shape the dish as they go. But it is the balance of the items they add and how they work them in the kitchen that influences the flavours and textures of the meal that reaches your table. And in brewing as in cooking, sometimes the best of intentions of the brewer/chef aren't enough to stop things from going wrong (see page 132). But let's start by looking at the basics of brewing – how the adventure begins...

MAKING BEER

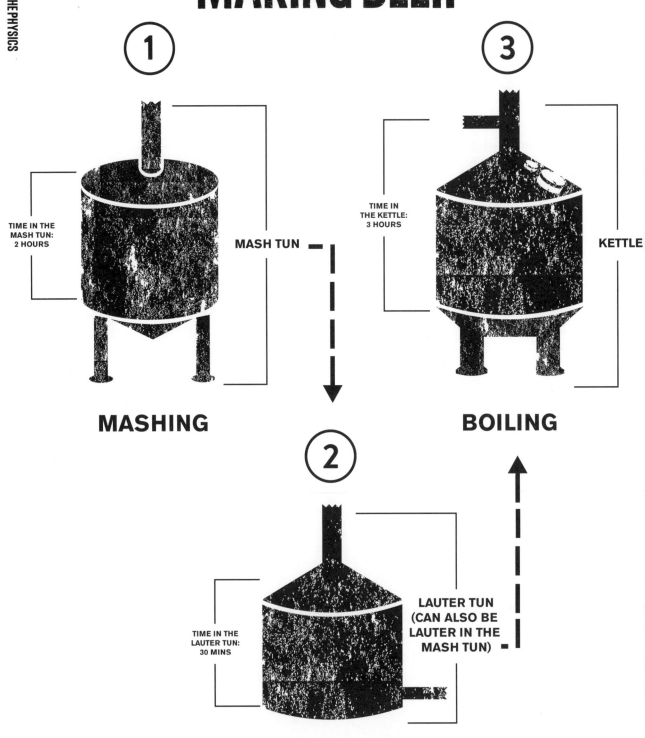

1

TIME IN THE
MASH TUN:
2 HOURS

MASH TUN

MASHING

2

TIME IN THE
LAUTER TUN:
30 MINS

LAUTER TUN
(CAN ALSO BE
LAUTER IN THE
MASH TUN)

LAUTERING

3

TIME IN
THE KETTLE:
3 HOURS

KETTLE

BOILING

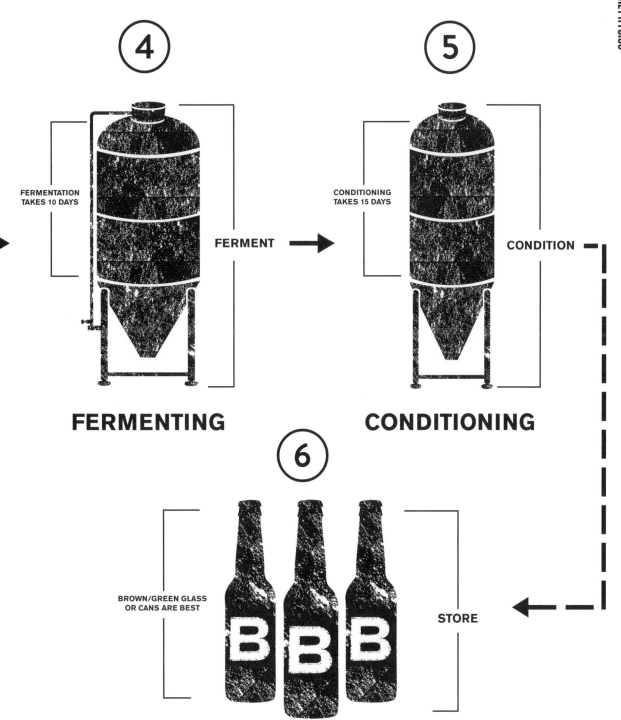

④ **FERMENTING**

FERMENTATION
TAKES 10 DAYS

FERMENT →

⑤ **CONDITIONING**

CONDITIONING
TAKES 15 DAYS

CONDITION

⑥ **BOTTLING**

BROWN/GREEN GLASS
OR CANS ARE BEST

STORE

OUR AVERAGE BEER IS MADE WITH OVER 40KG (88LB) OF MALTED BARLEY PER BARREL.

MASHING

Like any journey, brewing begins with a single step, which is to start the conversion of solid ingredients into the liquid that eventually graces your glassware. We'll take a closer look at the four pivotal building blocks of beer in a while (water, malt, hops and yeast), but every brew-day starts with the time-honoured task of mixing the first of those two in a process known as mashing. It involves pretty much what you'd expect given the name – the dry malted barley is combined with warm water – known as liquor – to form a glutinous porridge-like substance: the mash.

This is exactly what the brewer is after, and it forms very quickly indeed. The barley is partly crushed before it is soaked, and this cracking of the grains allows the warm water to get into each individual malt kernel and expose the starches within. The bottom line in brewing – the entire raison d'être – is to expose these starches and allow enzymes to convert them into sugars. Later on, the yeast the brewer adds will use these sugars as a food source and produce alcohol (and carbon dioxide), leading to the wondrous beer that sits before you now. You do have a beer, don't you?

LAUTERING

"SPENT" GRAIN THEREFORE ACTS AS ITS OWN FILTER, AIDING THE PROCESS.

OK, you're back. So the next step is to somehow separate this porridge and leave all the solids behind. This is done in a stage called lautering or sparging. More water is added to the top of the grain bed and allowed to percolate through, carrying the sweet sugars with it as it goes. The residual grains can actually help out here, as the barley husks lock together but allow liquid to flow round them (think pebbles in a stream, or coffee grounds). The so-called "spent" grain therefore acts as its own filter, aiding the process.

This step takes place either in the mash tun, or in a specially designed vessel called a lauter tun. Either way, the bottom of the container will have small holes to retain the solids but allow the liquid – now termed wort and commonly pronounced "wert" – to escape. Many brewers reintroduce the first part of the runnings back onto the top of the grain bed, as it will often contain a few husks and other unwanted particulates (this is known as re-circulation). Eventually the run-off is clear and is allowed to go on its way to the next stage of the brewing process…

IPA FANS, THIS IS THE TIME TO GET EXCITED, AS THE HOPS ARE READY TO GO.

BOILING

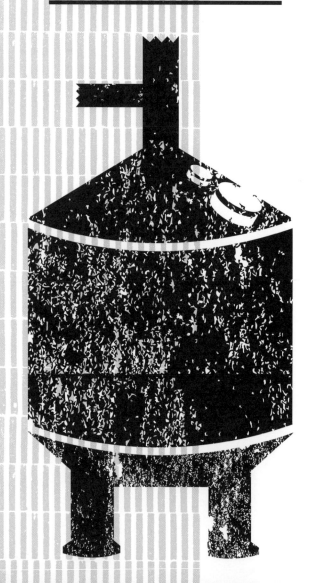

The wort is pumped into another large vessel and heated. It's not for nothing that this stainless-steel tank is known as the kettle. The liquid is boiled, with a vigorous rolling boil the desired outcome (we're not poaching eggs here). This prolonged heating stops dead the enzyme activity from the previous stages, giving the brewer a known quantity of sugars to move on to the next step, and it also sterilizes the wort to kill any bacteria that have been floating about – as we'll see later, although some brewers encourage bacteria to act on their beer, they only do it much later in the process. For now, the liquid that moves on to the fermentation stage has to be sterile.

One of the other reasons why brewers boil the wort relates to the next set of additions to the brew-day procedure: the third of beer's four of main ingredients. IPA fans, this is the time to get excited, as the hops are ready to go. Added to the boil in batches, carefully timed, the hops are "isomerized" by the heat – it rearranges their internal structure, releasing alpha and beta acids that make the beer heavy with aromas and long with taste-bud-prickling bitterness. The longer you boil them, the more of each you get, so brewers balance their requirements with these set additions – early batches give more bitterness, later additions are more for aroma and flavour.

BREWERS MAKE WORT, YEAST MAKES BEER.

FERMENTATION

The wort is then cooled and transferred once again, this time to a vessel (or vessels) where it will stay for a longer period. That's because it's time for the brewer to hand over his or her work to an army numbering in the tens of millions. Without yeast, all you'd be drinking would be thin, sweet cereal-water. With yeast, you get to drink beer. Once "pitched" into the fermentation vessel (or FV) the yeast gets to work, voraciously consuming the sugars the brewer has allowed to make it through the boil, converting their foodstuff of choice into ethanol and carbon dioxide. The power these simple fungi unleash is the most amazing part of the entire brewing process (the joke is that brewers make wort, yeast makes beer).

If you're lucky enough to visit a brewery, you can see this yeast-powered transformation happening before your eyes. Such is the appetite of the cells involved, and the nutrient-rich environment they have been introduced into, that the fermenting beer rises in great spumy clouds of foam and sometimes spills out of the vessel altogether. As we'll see shortly, there are hundreds of different strains of yeast – not just one. Each type has specific operating conditions the brewer needs to be aware of; and each brings a series of aroma and flavour characteristics that will alter the final beer in many different ways.

CONDITIONING

That's the reason why all this is performed, of course – to create a beverage with a flavour profile that makes people fall over themselves to drink it. And that is the aim of the final part of the brewing procedure, as the flavours develop and round out over time. The conditioning stage can last from a few days through to months, or even years. The brewery will retain the beer for as long as it takes for everything to reach a peak – the longer timespans of adding layers of flavour to a beer are up to you (see page 64 on how and why to "age" beer at home).

Before the final beer is packaged and shipped to your fridge or local bar of choice, the brewers need to ensure it is exactly as they wanted it. So the conditioning stage allows the yeasts to calm down fully and reabsorb some of the unwanted by-products they created during the furious initial moments of fermentation. It also gives them and accumulated proteins time to settle out in the tank and sink to the bottom – a process that can be aided by reducing the temperature (cold conditioning) or by introducing substances to cause these particulates to clump together and drift downward, so they can be left behind in the tank when the beer – it is actually beer now – is syphoned off and packaged.

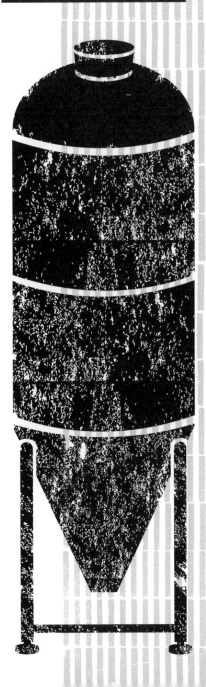

5AM SAINT

BITTERSWEET CHAOS

The origin of 5AM Saint's name is lost to history; an idea scribbled on a long-recycled jotter or hastily typed email that was dragged into a trash bin many moons ago. The rumour is that, back in the Fraserburgh days, it referred to the magical hour before dawn shift changeover, when the "5a.m. saints" arrived to relieve the overnighters, bearing bacon rolls and other early-morning sustenance for their fellow brewers.

At the same time, we were experimenting with a new dry-hopping regime for Punk IPA and realized that a similar process could transform our amber ale, The Physics. In a classic "brewhouse light-bulb moment", we found that applying these new, epic levels of dry hop utterly transformed the beer, and switching the base hops from UK varietals to their resinous, punchy North American cousins made it truly rock.

The result was a bitter twist on a classic style, taking the best characteristics of sweet malt and bitter hops and fusing them in perfect harmony. With a riot of citrus and berry aromas, the rejuvenated beer had a bold bitterness built against burnt-sugar sweetness, backed by dark fruit throughout. And with the piney hops coming to the fore alongside, we had found the perfect red ale.

But there was one more thing: this hopped-up newcomer needed a name. Although the finer points of the why and the how have fallen by the wayside, the 5a.m. saint designation seemed a perfect fit with a beer worthy of those who go the extra mile and also demand it of what they drink.

like that? try these:

BLAZING WORLD
6.8%

Modern Times, USA

Double IPA/Red Ale crossover, more hops in play as a result

LIQUID MISTRESS
5.8%

Siren Craft Brew, England

Citrus and dark raisin fruit come together in a true classic

TALL POPPY
7%

8 Wired, New Zealand

Perfect balance of sharp, fruity hops and caramel malt

AMERICAN RED ALE

RELEASED	2007
ABV	5%
STYLE	RED ALE
IBU	35
HOPS	CASCADE, AMARILLO, NELSON SAUVIN, SIMCOE, AHTANUM, CENTENNIAL
MALT	EXTRA PALE, CARA, MUNICH, CRYSTAL, DARK CRYSTAL

"5AM IS OUR HOMAGE TO THE RED ALES OF NORTH AMERICA — BEERS THAT PROVE IF YOU WANT HOPPY AND RESINOUS YOU DON'T AUTOMATICALLY HAVE TO GRAVITATE TOWARD IPAS OR EVEN GOLDEN BEERS. YOU CAN HAVE MALT AND HOPS AT THE SAME TIME..."
— MARTIN DICKIE

"5AM SAINT. MY FIRST BREWDOG BEER ON MY FIRST VISIT TO A BREWDOG BAR. IT WAS UNLIKE ANYTHING I'D TRIED BEFORE AND LED TO ME BECOMING A SHAREHOLDER. THIS BEER CHANGED MY LIFE." — EQUITY PUNK LLOYD WRIGHT

DROPTICK
TICK THIS BEER OFF YOUR LIST WITH A DROP FROM YOUR FINGER

YOU SAY:
....
....
....
....
....

THE
FUNDAMENTAL FOUR

IT ALL BEGINS IN A FIELD, FAR FAR AWAY. BEER IS
A BEVERAGE TO WHICH ANY NUMBER OF DIFFERENT
THINGS CAN BE ADDED — FROM CHILLI TO CHOCOLATE.
BUT AT ITS HEART IT CONTAINS A QUARTET OF KEY
INGREDIENTS, WITHOUT WHICH YOU WOULD BE
DRINKING SOMETHING VERY DIFFERENT INDEED.
LET'S TAKE A LOOK AT EACH OF THEM IN TURN...

THE FUNDAMENTAL FOUR:

MALT

It all begins in a field,
far far away...

Beer is, first and foremost, an agricultural product – the swaying golden landscape you see on walks in the countryside isn't just destined for flour mills and bread. These starchy grains are as perfect for brewers as they are for bakers, and the two industries have overlapped for centuries as a result. A number of different cereal crops are used in making beer and most – but not all – are processed beforehand to aid their effectiveness to the brewer. This procedure is known as malting, and we'll be taking a closer look at what it involves very shortly. But in terms of the actual grains in the brewer's arsenal, one in particular is king.

Rye, wheat, oats, rice and even corn can be added to the mash tun to begin a day's brewing, but by far the most crucial crop that brewers rely on is barley. The power of this incredible grain has been harnessed since Neolithic times, with wild seeds planted and tended by the very earliest of communities. Each tiny grain contains enzymes that work to convert its supply of starch into sugars: like a lunchbox making its own sandwiches. These days, barley is sown in two main forms based on the number of kernels that cluster around a central axis; two-row and six-row. This structural difference provides a very distinctive outlook when it comes to how they are used in brewing.

As you would expect given the numeric distinction, two-row barley has fewer kernels than six-row and therefore will yield not only less starch, but also fewer enzymes to do the grunt work. Despite this, its pleasingly symmetrical twinned kernels are more resistant to cold and dominate great swathes of the northern hemisphere. Six-row gives lots of everything to the brew – which can overload some brew-days but can be valuable to those whose beer making uses a lot of other, different grains that lack enough starch or enzymes of their own. This is a simple binary choice – how the barley is processed makes all the difference.

As brewers, we tend to rely on the catch-all term "malt" for the sacks of cereal that become the baseline of a beer, but this is actually an abbreviation of the technique that begins the entire brewing process (well, after planting and harvesting). Malting is the artificial germination of the tiny grains under controlled conditions – they are essentially tricked into germinating by being immersed in warm water. If left to its own devices, each barley grain would then use its internal starches to grow roots and shoots before producing a new plant – but the maltster wants to stop this conversion in good time, so that the majority of the starches are available to be used by brewers instead.

This partial germination releases enzymes inside each barley kernel, breaking down the internal structure and kicking off the conversion of carbohydrates into smaller starches, proteins and enzymes (this also makes the barley easier to crush, further aiding the brewer's work later in the process). The malt is then heated in a kiln, drying the grains out to arrest germination and fix the starches

THE MORE COMPLEX THE BEER, THE GREATER THE POTENTIAL NUMBER OF DIFFERENT MALTS.

in an exact ratio that the brewer can use to create specific beers. As we saw in the brewhouse boiling stage, enzymes are highly susceptible to heat, so the maltster treads a fine line between keeping the temperature so low that it halts their progress and ensuring they aren't denatured by the heat and ruined.

The kilning is highly controlled for another reason: how long the malt is roasted for has a huge impact on the flavours it imparts in the final beer. As you can imagine, grains roasted for a short time end up lighter in colour than those that undergo longer heating. This variation gives the brewers a huge number of malts to play with – from the pale ones with lightly toasty, biscuity flavours to the dark ones with characteristic chocolate and bitter coffee elements. Other varieties are roasted when wet to give a crystallized outer shell; these are universally known by another evocative flavour descriptor – caramel malt.

If we want to brew a pale ale, for instance, we largely mash in with pale malt, whereas a stout or a porter will contain a significant quantity of a dark malt. This is not as easy as it sounds, however; these darkly roasted malts have fewer enzymes and less starch remaining in their kernels, so we need to add some paler malt into the mash tun to help everything along. This is also true for caramel malts, as their crystallized sugars add sweetness and body to the final beer but only because these have become "unfermentable" – the yeast can't get at them and break them down. A lot of paler malt must be added alongside.

The more complex the beer, the greater the potential number of different malts involved to balance the flavours and yield enough for the yeast to work effectively. Beers like lagers will usually have a blend of only one or two different types of malt – whereas our barrel-aged Scotch ale Bourbon Baby contains a precise mix of (deep breath) extra-pale, Munich, dark crystal, Carafa, amber, brown and smoked malts plus wheat and flaked oats. These all bring something different to the party – extra-pale malt is the powerhouse, whereas smoked malt (produced by drying the barley over a wood-smoke fire) adds a touch of sweet, peaty woodiness. Each has a role to play!

As brewers, our jobs are made infinitely easier by the skill of the maltsters. Their ability to balance heat, moisture, time and varieties of grain into malt with known quantities means that we can brew the same beer time and again with very little variation, even if the cereal that arrives at the malthouse comes from different fields, or has been grown under varying conditions (as we get in Scotland, for instance). Just as importantly, it means when we experiment we can do so safe in the knowledge that the backbone of the beer will turn out a certain way – so when we change the techniques, add extra ingredients or age the beer in spirit casks we can be confident that the first part of the recipe is set – if not in stone, then in grain.

THE FUNDAMENTAL FOUR:

WATER

So without malt, you
would be drinking
something very different,
but without water, you'd
not be drinking anything
at all.

THE RESULT? THINK OF IRELAND, THINK OF STOUT.

Beer's most abundant ingredient also has an enormous impact on the final flavour – it is far more than a simple mechanism for delivering the other components. As well as leaching the all-important starches from the grains during the mashing-in phase of the brew-day, its impact on a beer is wide-reaching and fundamental. To get to grips with why and how it relates to the finished product, we are going to go back to school and talk about chemistry.

Of course, beer is almost all water, so water is going to have a huge impact on the work of the brewer – but the power it exerts is down to the chemicals and minerals the water molecules pick up from spending millennia underground or flowing through pipework running into the brewery. Whether dissolved and held in its structure for thousands of years or taken on board in a flash as it surges along a rusty conduit, what water brings with it has the potential to dramatically affect the taste of the beer when it has been packaged and sent to bars and shops months (or even years) later.

There are entire books devoted to this subject, but let's focus on three broad areas – pH, hardness and mineral content. The first of these – as every young chemistry student remembers – relates to whether a solution is acidic or alkaline and is something every brewery tests as a matter of course (albeit with something more technical than those little strips of colour-changing paper). The water in most cities leans toward the alkaline, and brewers need to be aware exactly how far it leans, because the pH of the mash will influence the colour, fermentability and – most importantly of all – the taste of the final beer.

Next up is hardness, although this is a measure of the mineral content, so these final two areas go hand in hand. Water leaches minerals from rocks and other naturally occurring sources, and the amounts of dissolved calcium or magnesium ions present will determine how "hard" the water is (high concentrations of minerals are said to result in hard water, low in soft water). Rocks like limestone contain a lot of calcium and pass these ions on to the water as it comes into contact and begins to dissolve it. This is important for brewing as it facilitates enzyme action and improves the ability of yeast to divide and flourish during the fermentation stage.

Calcium also lowers the pH of the mash by reacting with phosphates in the malt grains – this is a useful outcome that helps to counter the natural alkalinity of many brewhouse water sources – but it can go too far the other way. Hard alkaline water can also make the chemical compounds in hops taste overly bitter, so as we have seen at every other stage of the process the brewer needs a careful balancing act to ensure that the chemistry of the incoming water is as near ideal as possible, and that the various processes of the brew-day alter those factors in a beneficial, not a negative way. So what can brewers do to rein in the wildness of water, to adjust these parameters?

Simply put, they can embrace the science and adjust these factors by treating the water as they add it to the mash tun. For instance, if their domestic water is too soft, they can add something like gypsum to make it harder; if it's too hard, adding distilled water can regulate the chemistry in the other direction. This approach is sometimes a last resort – if the brewery is located in an area with a water chemistry that needs modification to bring out the best in the final beer – but sometimes brewers can switch up the composition of their starting liquid just because they want to. And that depends on what beer they are making.

As you can appreciate, this high-grade telemetry and laboratory analysis are relatively recent in the world of beer making. Before brewers truly understood the influence of chemistry on brewing – and, more importantly, were able to do something about it – they had to work out what styles of beer worked in their region and what didn't, and stick to those that succeeded. The great brewing cities of Munich and Vienna are known for their malty, amber beers (we'll come on to the specifics of beer styles later on) – this is, as much as anything else, because their alkaline water made it difficult to produce lighter beers.

In this way, water profiles shaped the brewing industries of entire countries. Take Ireland. Without too much thought we can all pinpoint a specific beer that flows from the Emerald Isle, and this is no coincidence. The rise of the dry Irish stout is a factor of the highly alkaline water that exists in Dublin, with concentrations of carbonate and calcium that needed to be balanced out in some way. Before chemical adjustment was an option, Irish brewers added a higher proportion of dark malt – which crucially is slightly acidic – to lessen the effect of their naturally occurring water. The result? Think of Ireland, think of stout.

Of course, stout – and particularly dry Irish stout – is a style that any brewer from Dublin to Dubai can make. Someone after the authentic version of that particular style can't easily import Irish water to produce a smooth, dark beer – but they can adapt the water profile to brew a beer that is fairly close to the real thing. Whether we're talking about the porters of London or the Pilsners of what is now the Czech Republic, it's now possible to produce the same style of beer halfway around the world due to our understanding of what water chemistry does in the brewing process, and how our experiment-loving brewers can embrace it and get their beers near enough to the classics.

THE FUNDAMENTAL FOUR:
HOPS

These mighty flowering cones are the reason your tongue delights in a lasting sensation of bitterness, just as they are the principal cause of the fruity, floral or piney aromas that lift from the surface of your beer, encouraging you to return for another taste.

Hops are another base ingredient that varies hugely depending on where they originate. They are the complex, pivotal components of all beers and have attracted the attentions of craft brewers like no other ingredient. The hoppy arms race is well and truly underway. Yet, for a long time, hops weren't used for flavour, if at all. Hops have been grown specifically for use in brewing for over a thousand years; adding them to beer acts as a preservative, keeping the final product stable for longer. Wild hops were used before that (they commonly grow as climbing plants in temperate regions). Further back, early brewers who were unaware of or unable to use hops added different herbs or other plants instead, such as bog myrtle (also known as sweet gale and used extensively in early Scottish brewing). Belgian brewers used a mixture of herbs known as gruit, of which myrtle was a chief ingredient – this blend was so vital and ubiquitous that the owner of the trading rights usually became very wealthy.

Hops and "terroir"

Hops provide the aromas and flavours in your beer in a similar way to grapes in wine – with the chief and important difference that, unlike grapes, hops do not contain the fermentable sugars used by the yeast (as we've seen, this is one of the main reasons why malts are added). They are dioecious – both male and female plants exist – and it is the cones of the female plants that are used to produce beer. These cones are harvested, dried and then sold to brewers as they are (hop flowers) or compacted into hop pellets. It's a brewer's choice as to which they use, as both have advantages and disadvantages – many craft breweries use a mixture depending what beer is on the brew-sheet.

Speaking about wine (we have to, every now and again) leads us to consider a feature of hops that is very much the go-to concept of the grape-based medium – terroir. The influence of the soils, climate and growing aspect is well advertised for wine, and it works in exactly the same way for beer. The many varietals of hops – now well over a hundred different types, and increasing – equate to a wide range of different flavours and aromas, and this is in large part down to the specific part of the world where the hop bine (not vine) breaks through the earth and begins its upward journey. So let's take a look at some of the more common hop regions of the world, and their associated characters.

From the hop-growing lowlands of England come an assortment of varietals such as Fuggles and East Kent Goldings that are earthy, spicy and give off aromas like fresh-cut grass on a rainy afternoon. (These kinds of tasting notes make beer sound like wine, but are essential to describe and relate the different beers to new drinkers – the real reason they exist in the wine industry. It's not to elevate the drink to a more classy echelon.) Across in the heart of Europe is the home of the "noble" hops – Germanic strains like Saaz and Hallertauer that are herbal and floral. In far-distant New Zealand there are Nelson Sauvin and Motueka, limy, vinous and giving aromas similar to the best Marlborough white wines. And in the USA there are the high-citrus, high-pine thunderbolts such as Simcoe, Ahtanum and Amarillo that leave the tongue tingling with resin or pithy fruit (orange, for instance, in the case of Amarillo).

THE HOPPY ARMS RACE IS WELL AND TRULY UNDERWAY.

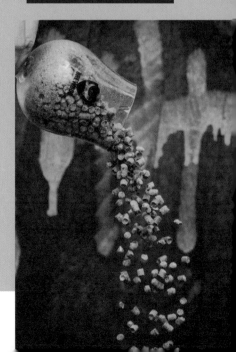

As we've seen, brewers adapt the water to suit the beer they are creating, then use a blend of differently treated malts to build the baseline – but it is the hops that truly influence the final aromas and flavours of the beer. And aroma and flavour are very distinct aspects – some hops are used for their properties on the nose, others for how they interact with your taste buds. Saaz is a perfect example of an aroma hop; the noble variety transfers its classic spiciness into the first few whiffs of a Pilsner. Conversely, the kiwi Waimea is a bittering hop that packs a punch of pine and citrus and is used – for brewers who can get hold of it – to deploy in lip-smacking pale ales and IPAs.

And that is a fact of modern beer making. Hops are in, and when anything becomes a much sought-after commodity one of two things immediately happens: they become harder to acquire as the word gets out, and their price rises as a result. Modern craft brewers typically enter into hop contracts months or years in advance to guarantee their supply and keep that specifically hopped beer in their line-up. The fact that hops are often susceptible to non market-based issues such as disease and varied rainfall only compounds the potential headaches for brewers.

As we saw in the section on the boil during the brew-day, the different hops that go into a recipe are added at different times to make full use of their individual properties. The first additions provide bitterness, so the big hitters that can take a longer boil are tipped into the kettle first. As the heating stage continues, flavour hops are added and then finally those that contribute more delicate aromas. The oils in the hops are volatile and are boiled off, which is why those that contain smaller amounts (the aroma hops) are added last. Brewers also add hops to the conditioning stage, and this "dry-hopping" intensifies the aroma and flavour yet further.

THE FUNDAMENTAL FOUR:
YEAST

The brewer is still
far from done, but when
it comes round to the
final member of our
fantastic foursome we
will gladly take a back
seat. What takes over
next is something that
has a huge influence
on how you perceive
a particular beer.

Yeasts are truly astonishing micro-organisms, and it's no exaggeration to say they have played a pivotal role in human society. Ancient Egypt – the breadbasket of antiquity – had its foundations underpinned by the frothing top layer of brewing pots that was skimmed and used to leaven flour and water into bread with its bubbles.

For hundreds of years people embraced yeast without knowing what it was – its secrets weren't revealed until the golden age of chemistry in the mid-to-late nineteenth century. Early brewers simply found a process that worked and repeated it, and the unseen micro-organisms worked away on their behalf. In Egypt, for example, brewers introduced the end of one brew into the start of the next, maintaining the cycle of fermentation. The Nordic countries had a typically Viking attitude – passing down beer-stirring sticks as miracle heirlooms (that happened to harbour billions of yeast cells in the wood).

Many brewers just stared into their foaming brewing vessels and believed that what they were witnessing was a case of divine intervention. What none of them could realize was that wild yeasts were responsible, having been present in their wooden vats or simply wafting in on the breeze to act on their brew in a timely manner. These wild yeasts are microscopic fungi carried on the air, settling wherever fate takes them – you are almost certainly covered in them now. When that particular play of chance results in them arriving into a warm, starchy liquid, then they multiply at an insane rate, feasting on the bounty and producing alcohol and carbon dioxide.

Although there are well over a thousand recorded species of yeast, only a few have what it takes to produce this favourable outcome, and they are collectively known as brewing yeasts. Individual strains are identified, propagated and then cared for by brewers for generations – of yeasts and brewers alike – as each produces a distinctive flavour profile that can be picked up by the drinker once the final beer has been packaged. One brewery's "house" yeast can yield very different results to another's, and brewers become attuned to their billions of tiny helpers, and know fairly accurately how the beer will turn out.

Human overlords aside, yeasts display at least one streak of individuality: where in the brewing vessel they do their work. Beer-friendly microbes roughly group into top-fermenting and bottom-fermenting yeasts. This is as simple as it sounds – some ferment on the surface of the wort and stay there, while others sink to the depths once they are done. The first are often known as ale yeasts – such as the commonly used *Saccharomyces cerevisiae* – and the latter lager yeasts, headed up by *Saccharomyces pastorianus*. Real life is never as binary as that, of course; some ale yeasts end up at the bottom of the tank too.

Speaking of lager, the one thing we all know about it is its association with cold – served from fridges, giving refreshment on hot days, adverts with shards of ice, and so on. The yeasts that work to form this family of beers can do so at cooler temperatures than ale yeast, meaning lagers can be produced in colder brewhouses to give a different flavour profile: cleaner and lacking the fruitier esters that give ales their characteristic floral spicy taste.

IT'S NO EXAGGERATION TO SAY THAT YEASTS HAVE PLAYED A PIVOTAL ROLE IN HUMAN SOCIETY.

The cut-off is around 13°C (55°F) – under that most ale yeasts simply can't get going, whereas lager yeasts will thrive into the single figures Celsius (below 48°F) and yield a beer that can be conditioned at very low temperatures to ensure its flavour holds up.

So how exactly does yeast work? Well, entire degree courses are devoted to this subject, and without a second volume of this book on the chemistry of fermentation, we are going to have to be very brief on the wondrous process. Yeast cells added into the wort – usually unceremoniously dumped into the tank via a bucket – voraciously take up the food supply and begin to reproduce; they are in the perfect environment. Enzymes within their cells convert fermentable sugars in the wort into glucose, which they in turn convert into ethyl alcohol and carbon dioxide. Many other by-products that can influence the taste of the beer also result – but let's leave it at that for now.

As the yeasts flurry through the food supply and reproduce with abandon, the concentrations of what they are outputting also rise. This inevitable truth spells the beginning of their end, as in an unfortunate paradox alcohol is toxic to yeast, once it reaches a certain level. The yeast becomes dormant, and fermentation is over. This moment is reached faster if the ambient temperature is higher, but as we have seen yeasts are vulnerable to this as well – too low and they can't function properly, too high and they can actually be killed. They walk a fine line throughout; the brewer has to be aware of their limitations.

This is the great thing about each brewery having a "house strain" – those who work with the yeast every day soon learn exactly how it behaves, and can dial in each parameter accordingly. They – and the drinker – will be rewarded with a beer characteristic with flavours such as banana and clove (typically for Belgian-style beers), peppery spice, floral notes or a complex array of different fruity esters. Beyond the influence of the malt, the hops and any other ingredients the brewer adds, it is billions of single-celled organisms that have the greatest effect on what you taste when you have that first sip of beer.

FRESHNESS

How do you know when a beer is good? Well, the great thing about brewing is that any brewer worth their salt won't release a beer unless it is. It's like chefs tasting everything at the pass; they know how the recipe should taste, and if it doesn't meet their criteria (born of years of practice combined with their own sense of pride) then it doesn't go out. Beer is the same. And brewers have a distinct advantage – the conditioning phase, as discussed on page 45. Chefs must turn their orders around as fast as possible. Brewers have a glorious buffer of time as the beers develop their layers of aroma and flavour.

In reality, it's a complicated process – every large metal tank of developing beer that isn't-quite-there-yet is a vessel that the brewers can't be filling with the next batch of something equally exciting. But the best brewers are adept at this plate-spinning routine, and once the contents of a tank has passed its final taste test and flavour analysis then it's good to go. And from that moment, the beer is at its peak. We'd jetpack ours to you, if it meant it got there quicker (and if we could get our hands on a jetpack). With a few exceptions – see overleaf – as soon as a beer leaves a brewery it is only going to get worse. When it comes to craft beer, freshness is king. But why?

Because of the twin pillars of craft beer, that's why. The malt and hops in a beer provide its personality, individuality and – of course – aroma and flavour, and they are on the clock. Hop oils that survive vanishing into the ether during the boil will degrade over time once the beer has been packaged. Proteins from the malt grains that give a beer its body will deteriorate. The stale, musty flavours heralding the influx of oxygen will increase. These things happen in that order, so pale ales and other hop-forward beers will go south first, their peaks of citrus and resin decreasing. Fresh beer is tastier.

So if you see a beer in a shop, check the expiry date. The later the better, for hoppy beers, as it indicates they have left the brewery and arrived on the shelves more recently. Some breweries have adopted the "bottled on" dating system, which is the best indication you can hope for. Not only does it show that the producer takes freshness seriously, it will tell you exactly when the brewer determined their creation was at its peak. If you can get hold of it within days or weeks, then lucky you – pick it up, take it home, let it rest and chill a little and then taste it – short of speaking to the brewers personally this is the closest you'll get to discovering how their mind works…

AGEING GRACEFULLY

So let's imagine that you've returned from a successful mission to the local shop. Or maybe you've just had a beer order delivered and are standing up to your ankles in packaging chips. Unless there's a group of people applauding and reaching for the bottle opener, chances are you're not going to drink every one of your purchases right away.

So what's the best place to store the newly arrived beer? And how long can you keep it?

The short answer is to fire everything into the fridge. An initial period of refrigeration allows the beer to recover from its journey, and any sediment from bottle-conditioning to settle out to the bottom. Chilling beer is the perfect method for retaining flavour (it's one of the reasons why draft beer is served cool). This is because heat is bad news for beer – it destroys the protein configurations that give the liquid body, flavour and condition.

So cold is good. But unless you have a dedicated beer fridge – in which case kudos to you – what's the alternative for long-term storage? To avoid temptation and keep the beer for a while, store it upright in a cool, dark place. Ideal locations could be a spare kitchen cupboard away from appliances (and prying hands), or an attic that faces away from the prevailing sunshine. Or better yet, a cellar. There's a reason wine people use them; and it's not just that the spiders prevent you from venturing inside and discovering their secrets.

Age catches up with us all eventually, and beer is no different. The flavour profile will alter. The citrus and resinous peaks of the hops will fade, the malt flavours gradually change from earthy bitterness into a sweeter place altogether – and eventually the entire beer will succumb to oxidation and become dulled, with the overriding sensation of papery drabness that will make you do a double-take at the label promising flashing hop flavour and warning you that the beer will pummel your taste buds.

So why would you ever want to experience this?

Because, for some beers, leaving them alone in a cool dark place for a few months – or even years – will yield far more complex flavours when the time comes to open them up. Beer-ageing helps soften and round out harsh flavours, while letting others mature over time. As a rough rule of thumb, for ageing beer successfully it helps if your purchase fits these particular set of characteristics…

1. HIGH ABV

Just think of the drinks that people typically keep in their cellar (those who are lucky enough to have one). Wine; whiskies, maybe. Although the latter won't improve unless they are in a cask (in the cellar of someone who is truly lucky), they will last a long time. And like wine, they have a double-digit ABV. So it follows with beer. Higher levels of alcohol in your bottle will become mellower as they act to preserve the beer, countering the effects of oxygen as they go. Anything around or north of 8% ABV has a great chance of standing the test of time.

2. LOW HOPS

With a few exceptions – there are always exceptions – beers that pack in the hops aren't good prospects for your cellar. We'll talk about Double IPAs in a moment, but by and large those that advertise citrus and resin levels to take the enamel off your teeth are best enjoyed right away. With the hop character fading and becoming more dulled over time, try to select styles that major on malt or have interesting yeast qualities. Hop bombs fall flat if they are concealed for any length of time, so saddle them up, don't cellar them away.

3. BOTTLE-CONDITIONED

Here's another mention of the conditioning phase (have we imparted how important it is to the brewer yet?): one nifty trick is that by adding a small amount of yeast to the bottle, the brewers can prolong this phase after the beer has left their facility. Bottle-conditioned beers maintain their flavour longer as the tiny yeast cells consume sugars present in the beer and kick out carbon dioxide. This will keep the sealed beer carbonated for longer, meaning when the big day comes you'll have a hiss of satisfaction and not a flat, dull waste of time in your hands.

So given these rules of thumb, certain styles will greet you in a new light when given the benefit of a little extra on the meter. If you have any of these in your collection, and a fair amount of patience, here's what you could be in for…

BARLEY WINES

Although they aren't as dark as stouts, barley wines are built from the malt base upward – in fact, they are mostly malt base – so unfurl as they age. These are the beers to uncork and drink in your armchair, as they take oxidation in their stride, leaving you with a robust, sherry-like beer. Swirl in your favoured goblet by the fire.

BELGIAN BEER

Anything goes in the Low Countries, as we shall see, and the funky, yeast-heavy sour beers of Belgium are incredible to age – they get softer, sweeter and fruitier. So too are the Trappist beers, as they often hit all three of the tick-boxes on the previous pages, being barely hopped, bottle-conditioned and strong enough to put hairs on your chest. They age beautifully.

IMPERIAL IPA

These are the exceptions to the rule of hops – but only because of their malt backbone. The hop notes will indeed fall away with time, but as they do will be replaced by sweeter caramel and toffee flavours from the malt bill. Released from its partner's demise, the malt-heavy double or imperial IPAs become fascinating when aged.

IMPERIAL STOUTS

Big, dark and roasty, these beers typically have a high success rate when aged; their flavours become more relaxed and verge into sweeter milk chocolate, dried figs or other fruit, or a deeply roasted coffee. With low hop levels and typically high alcohol, these are the poster-children for ageing beer.

Whatever you decide to store away, your reward is right there developing under your roof. When the time comes, buy a recent version of what you are about to taste and open them side by side – that is when you'll truly be able to notice just how, if left to their own devices, some beers can age gracefully and take on a whole new set of flavours.

BARREL AGEING
THE MAGIC & MYSTERY OF WOOD

Ageing doesn't just take place in the attics, cellars and garages of beer fans. One of the biggest trends in craft beer involves the brewers shouldering that responsibility themselves, before the beer ever reaches their customers. In a rather neat throwback, the methods they use hark back to some of the earliest days of brewing. Applying a little bit of science, a modicum of good fortune and a spot of astute recycling, brewers are pulling flavours from one of the original storage mediums for beer and bringing it into the modern era. Barrel-aged beer is quite simply beer production elevated into an art form.

And the reason is that to create these beers, brewers have to overrule their own instinct. Brewers have to be clean freaks. Bacteria are the enemy. Wild yeasts (unless you're brewing certain Belgian-style beers) are to be avoided at all costs. Each piece of equipment needs to be sterile – everyone washes up after dinner, but brewers have to wash their dishes before use as well. Only greenhorns go into the industry thinking it's about the latest amazing hops and dreaming up astonishing new recipes. Well, it is, but only after you've done your chores. And yet, we have barrel-ageing. The conditioning phase is completed away from the safe, sterile environs of a stainless-steel tank; the beer is decanted into old wooden barrels.

Many barrels still slosh with the dregs of the previous occupants: whisky or bourbon, sherry, red wine. Brewers sanitize their kit, tick every box, then fight against every sense by placing their creation in the hands of Father Time, ensconced in wood. It was the vagaries of barrel-use that led to the industry-wide adoption of stainless steel in the first place – why would brewers want to bring them back? Well, as with anything else to do with craft beer, the answer is flavour. Whatever was in the cask before will have left its mark in the wood, and there's the toasting of the barrel for wine, or the charring for bourbon. Or the wild bacteria, lurking in every nook and cranny.

To sum it up, barrel-ageing is an educated crapshoot. The moment you pipe in your freshly brewed beer, a number of things can happen – and not all of them are good. The flavour, the strength will both change beyond measure – Scotch whisky casks can yield smoky, peaty flavours; American bourbon, vanilla, oaky notes. Red wine casks give huge amounts of dark berry fruit and tannins. White wine can impart vinous, gooseberry dryness to a beer.

And these days the more adventurous wood-agers are experimenting with everything up to and including tequila barrels. Anything that can pass on a flavour is fair game.

And then there are sours. We'll talk about this fantastic, fearless style at length later – but the new prevalence of tart, dry and puckering beers is often linked with barrels. Enormous oak foudres, as used by the lambic breweries and blenders of Belgium and the craft breweries of North America, provide a tailor-made location for the bacteria that work their souring magic on a sugar-rich beer. Once the beer has been inside for long enough, it is removed and the bacteria and wild yeasts coating the sides remain there for the next arrival.

At this stage, you may wonder how the brewer knows what's going on inside the barrel. The flavours don't flip instantly – these things take time. So how do they know when sufficient time has elapsed? Well, the answer is the obvious one: they taste the contents. Constantly. If you have a barrel store like ours or those of other big barrel-ageing fanatics, there could be up to (and above) several hundred in there. Barrel masters very quickly develop a tuned sense of smell and taste to determine how their creations are doing, and when to pull the plug (or bung).

TO SUM IT UP, BARREL-AGEING IS AN EDUCATED CRAPSHOOT.

The Rock Star Gueuzestekers

The true masters of this difficult art are the lambic blenders of Belgium. This style of spontaneously fermented beer was historically either aged by the brewers themselves or sent to a specialist blender to curate for them. Many breweries didn't have the space for the colossal oak foudres. The experts at breweries like Boon or Drie Fonteinen have spent entire careers judging when a beer is ready to be released (as a lambic) or when the cask has given a different flavour and would be better blended. These mixes of old and young lambic are known

as *gueuze* (or *geuze*, depending on where you are) – and they are, in a word, stunning.

The *gueuzestekers*, or blenders, know the characteristics of every cask in their possession – their livelihoods depend on it. They also know that each time the foudre is filled the results will be slightly different. The degree of blending – or whether the cask is good to go as is – is entirely their decision. And to get to this level, they taste the contents of their barrel store every day. Their charges are kept at a constant temperature so as not to lead to fluctuations that could affect the beer inside. In that respect, they are more like farmers than brewers – tending a crop, working with the seasons, minimizing the play of chance.

And they are truly historic too. Take Brouwerij Boon, located in the small Belgian town of Lembeek. Owner Frank Boon has been brewing lambic and blending it into gueuze since 1975. In two colossal rooms at his brewery sit 130 wooden foudres, collectively holding the largest stock of lambic in Belgium – in all, 1.6 million litres (423,000 gallons) of fermenting beer. Each one contains an average of 8,000 litres (2,100 gallons) of beer and they are so individual that Frank and his team know where each one came from and how old it is. And the very oldest is cask number 79. It was hammered together somewhere in France in the mid-1800s, using oak timbers that at the time were almost 250 years old. Fittingly, it is used to store some of Frank's longest-kept lambic.

If those hundreds of years slip over your head, consider this. Every time you drink a glass of Boon Geuze Mariage Parfait, a beer which is created out of 5% young fresh lambic blended with 95% lambic aged three years or over (in cask number 79), you will be tasting beer that came into contact with wood that germinated from acorns in the 1670s, when Charles II and Louis XIV were on their respective thrones. Just a handful of years after the English captured and renamed New Amsterdam after their patron, the Duke of York. Barrel-aged beers have a complexity, a depth, a character – and above all, a history – that are unsurpassed in the beer world.

PARADOX

THE BEER THAT PRECEDED BREWDOG

We don't play favourites with our line-up of beers: affection runs deep for each and every BrewDog release. But there are some entries in our brewing schedule that draw the eye a little quicker – those that embrace experimentation, for instance, or are placed into the flavour-changing unpredictability of barrels. Or even those that pre-date the founding of our company altogether. Like Paradox.

Our ongoing investigation into barrel-ageing, the Paradox series began in Martin's garage long before there even was a BrewDog. An imperial stout he added to an old Islay cask (yes, he had a whisky cask in his garage), it was one of the beers we gave to legendary beer writer Michael Jackson to get an opinion in that life-changing meeting back in 2007.

Without Paradox there would be no BrewDog, it's that simple. Consigning our imperial stout to different ex-spirit barrels for months (or even years) showcases the art of barrel ageing. The influence that each beer receives is represented in the beer name; look for Paradox Jura, the intense Paradox Smokehead or to other horizons such as Bourbon and even Rum. Each picks up flavours present in the wood and changes utterly in the process.

This goes against every fibre of our beings as brewers. We clean, sanitize and ensure we know 100% what is going into our beer, what it comes into contact with and therefore how it will taste when ready. But as soon as we then tip it into an old whisky barrel, all bets are off. We don't even know when we will be able to release it again. Only the barrel does. And that is the biggest brewing Paradox of all.

RAIN SHADOW

10%

Buxton Brewery, England

Rain Shadow took eight months to perfect – and is dark, deep and intense

THE ABYSS

11%

Deschutes Brewery, USA

Liquorice and molasses take this barrel-aged stout to another level

KENTUCKY BREAKFAST STOUT

11.2%

Founders Brewing Company, USA

Bourbon-aged stout the makers describe as "backwoods pleasure without the banjo"

BARREL AGED STOUT

RELEASED	2007
ABV	VARIES
STYLE	BARREL-AGED IMPERIAL STOUT
IBU	VARIESF
HOPS	VARIES
MALT	VARIES
EXTRAS	BARREL-AGEING

"PARADOX REPRESENTS EVERYTHING THAT WE LOVE ABOUT BREWING, AND EVERYTHING THAT BREWDOG STANDS FOR. IT'S INNOVATIVE, UNCOMPROMISING AND PUSHES THE BOUNDARIES AS TO WHAT BEER IS."

— MARTIN DICKIE

"I LOVE THE PARADOX SERIES AS IT'S AN OPENER TO THE DIFFERENT STYLES OF WHISKY AND THE CHARACTER EACH ONE HOLDS, AND A GREAT WAY TO INTRODUCE BEER DRINKERS TO WHISKY AND VICE VERSA."

— EQUITY PUNK MARK LAMBERT

DROPTICK

TICK THIS BEER OFF YOUR LIST WITH A DROP FROM YOUR FINGER

YOU SAY:

....
....
....
....
....
....

BOTTLES

POUR YOUR BOTTLE INTO A GLASS FOR BEST RESULTS!

Beer's most commonly found container has a huge effect on how you perceive the liquid inside; there's much more to the humble glass bottle than meets the eye. First introduced in 17th-century England, bottles were initially hugely expensive ways to carry your beer around. Early problems with pressure and carbonation blowing the top off were dealt with, and corks eventually gave way to caps as mass-production arrived. It may have taken 300 years, but the 20th century was the time when bottled beer well and truly hit the mainstream.

PROS

PORTABILITY – easy to package in groups and carry around…

DARK GLASS – brown bottles cut out 98% of the wavelengths of light that cause beer spoilage…

BOTTLE-CONDITIONING – great for adding a slug of yeast to continue to protect the beer's flavour…

EASY TO RECYCLE – accepted in recycling bins all over the world.

PITFALLS

CLEAR GLASS – clear glass offers zero protection against "skunky" wavelengths of light which can damage the beer's aroma and flavour…

CHILL – although bottled beers stay cold for longer, if you like them on the cooler side, it takes a while…

WEIGHT – the heaviness of bottles increases transport costs for breweries and makes carrying them home harder…

EASY DRINKERS – avoid the temptation to drink from the bottle – the aromas and flavours won't be as good!

CANS

NO LIGHT? NO OXYGEN? NO BEER-QUALITY PROBLEMS!

Canned beer follows the same principles but in a smaller, neater package. First sold to customers between World Wars I and II, the metal can's portability has won fans across the world. Originally unsealed with a "church key" opener (so-called because it resembled one of those heavy-duty keys wielded by monks), as technology progressed so too did the numbers of canned-beer drinkers. The craft beer industry has rediscovered cans with a vengeance, and now any high-end shop will have at least several of these new interlopers hiding amid the bottled ranks.

PROS

PORTABILITY – lighter and easier to open than bottles, the perfect package for beer on the go…

ZERO LIGHT – with no light able to broach their metal cloak, cans are ideal for keeping damaging rays at bay…

THE ENVIRONMENT – cans don't break and leave shards everywhere and have lower transport costs…

EASY TO RECYCLE – aluminium is "infinitely recyclable" – it can be turned into a new can with no loss of quality.

PITFALLS

THINNESS – cans cool down in a fraction of the time of bottles, but also warm up faster…

LESS VARIETY – cans come in fewer sizes and styles than bottles, giving you fewer options to pick from…

PERCEPTION – cans are seen as being for "cheap beer" and imparting a metallic taste to the final product – neither is true!

CASKS

HARD TO MASTER, BUT REWARDING!

If you're reading this outside the UK, your path may not cross that of cask ale on a regular basis – and this is an undoubted shame. Casks may be hard to look after and suit only a certain range of beer types, but when done well the medium allows beer to be presented at its absolute best. The beer continues to condition inside the vessel and is tapped and served as soon as it is ready; it's then drunk with the utmost speed before oxygen dulls the flavours and the condition wanes. But this is beer as it used to be – served via hand pump without extraneous carbon dioxide, but with just the right amount of carbonation, foamy head and conversation about the weather.

KEGS

TOO GOOD TO STAND ON AT PARTIES!

Outside the UK, the keg has the upper hand. Pressurized systems rush beer from the containers to the bar fonts, and then into your glass. Using carbon dioxide or nitrogen (or a combination of both), the beer arrives carbonated and ready to go. Kegged beer systems make up for the old-fashioned complexity of cask with a futuristic complexity of their own, involving glycol chillers, humming generators and fan systems. With several different types of kegs on the market (from different countries), bar staff have to be aware which is which and have the appropriate connectors on hand to be able to free the beer – under controlled conditions – from its steely embrace.

PROS

MOUTHFEEL – a well-cellared and poured cask pint is smooth, light and in perfect condition…

STYLE COUNCIL – for bitters, pale ales and stouts, the cask is an ideal way to highlight the nuances…

SENT PACKING – beers are racked into casks before conditioning is complete; this clears space in the brewhouse vessels for more…

TRADITION – keeping alive the history and tradition of the UK's native style of storing and serving beer.

PROS

LONG LASTING – usually a lot longer than cask, because the keg keeps oxygen ingress at bay…

REUSABLE – kegs (like casks) are sent back to the brewery to be cleaned, refilled and dispatched once again…

CARBONATION – gas mixtures can be set religiously. If a brewer has a specific requirement, the drinker will receive it…

STYLE COUNCIL – kegging is perfect for styles with lots of hops or sourness, or more wine-like beers.

PITFALLS

DRINK FAST – once tapped, a cask has only a few days of life before the beer begins to lose condition…

WARM UP – the ideal temperature range is between chilled and room temperature, requiring careful monitoring…

BREWER'S LOT – your carefully made beer is (literally) in the hands of others to serve well or serve badly…

KEEP STILL – move or knock the cask and risk muddying the beer with the settled yeast and other solids.

PITFALLS

CHILL OUT – storage and transit are done at colder temperatures than cask – a warning for anyone with sensitive teeth…

CLEAN FREAK – the metres of pipework, nozzles, dials and taps all need careful cleaning to kill spoiling bacteria…

FIZZZZZ – if kinks in the line or gas problems occur, your beer will be replaced in the glass by a spluttering of foam…

COUPLING – using different kegs requires a skilful cellarperson and plenty of different couplers to connect them.

CRAFT
ON DECK

DRINKING IN STYLE

So, let's crack open the largest multi-pack of beers ever and see what's inside. Over the next few pages we'll look at the many different types of craft beer – from crisp, floral lagers to dusky imperial stouts that taste of 20 different things at once. But with so much variety, how can you possibly narrow down what to drink? Is there a way to group beers into different stables to give a rough idea of what flavours result if you pick a particular door?

Yes – and that is the beauty of the beer style.

Like many things, this term is thanks to the Beer Hunter, Michael Jackson, who did more to wake the world up to beer than any other since the war. Way before we crossed his radar, our early advocate recognized that to get people interested in drinking beer, you have to let them quantify the available options. So he introduced, and popularized, beer styles.

"There is not merely 'French wine', but a whole range of classic styles, from Champagnes to Clarets to Sauternes," Michael wrote on his website, *Beer Hunter Online* in 2003. "You want brandy? Armagnac, Cognac, Calvados, an Alsatian 'white alcohol' distilled from pears, plums or some obscure berry…" He knew that brewing had just as much – if not more – diversity than anything that started life in a vineyard or orchard, and realized that for people to become enthused about beer the word had to get out.

Let's take one of his favourites – the Flanders Red. He once described the "world-class" beers of Rodenbach and other producers in a small area as "a distinct style without a name" – but by referring to the "red beers" produced by these great breweries of West Flanders in Belgium, he helped popularize a collective term for them. So now if a drinker spies Flanders Red on a beer menu, if they've had one before they will summon those flavours in their head once again (and anybody who has tried a Flanders Red will very much have a set of flavours in their head, take it from us).

As more people take an interest in beer, the people who produce it have realized that descriptive terms and umbrella styles are more and more useful. Bigger breweries reliant on branding (think of a beer commercial and at least one name will pop into your head) are losing out to the modern upstarts of the craft beer industry precisely because of this work that people like Michael Jackson began all those years ago. Break it down for them. If they get a taste for what they discover are Schwarzbiers, then they will seek yours out.

Of course the elephant in the room is that the experimental nature of modern beermaking is pulling these traditional styles apart at the seams. Nothing insists style should be adhered to – only that it should be respected. The world of brewing is very different from what it was in the 1980s; chances are if you pick up four Berliner Weisse from your local craft outlet, at least two of them will have an unusual ingredient in the recipe, or be stronger than they typically are, or barrel-aged or whatever. And that leads to issues, particularly when judging these beers in competitions.

Then, the s-word gains a dreaded prefix as the great and the good peer into a glass held at eye height and ponder if it is "to style". Can an American porter contain pecans? Should a British brown ale be brewed over 6% ABV? Why would you make a pomegranate Gose? Well, the simple answer is the classic Mount-Everest-climbing response: why the heck not? If we as brewers revel in an industry that doesn't hold us back, what's to stop us from putting our individuality on the beers we create? Make them unique.

Styles are a fantastic guide for people looking to try new things, or sticking to what they already know – and that is all. So on the following pages we'll dissect the intricacies of many of the world's great beer styles, but chances are examples exist that contain all manner of other things as well. We think that's alright. We would hope that Michael Jackson would have shared that opinion. Beer styles are like building blocks – there for support, and to be relied on, but ultimately a tool of the architect's imagination.

And when it comes to craft beer, one style is king…

THE RISE OF IPA

Variety is the spice of life, so the saying goes, and craft brewers embrace this every time they mash in. The range of different beer styles (including spiced beers) is vast, with new variations and permutations invented every week by brewers putting twists on old favourites. But in craft beer, one particular style rules them all – the India Pale Ale.

More than ABV, IBU or OMG the most important three-letter acronym in modern brewing is IPA. If craft beer is for the people, then IPA is for its true disciples. It is of-the-moment like no other beer, and symbolizes both the desire of beer fans to seek out highly hopped alternatives to what they were drinking previously and the shift of outlook in breweries to keep them supplied with the pale and hoppy.

As Garrett Oliver, brewmaster of the Brooklyn Brewery in New York, is fond of summarizing, "When I started out, IPA was a traditional English style brewed by nobody. Now it is an American style brewed by everybody." That sentiment hints at the biggest irony of all – as British craft beer drinkers are won over by the power of the hop, they are actually drinking a beer style that began life in their very own country.

The exact time and place the beer that became India Pale Ale was first brewed in the UK has been lost to history, but brewers have been selling pale ale – beer brewed with a significant proportion of pale malt – in London since the turn of the 18th century. The true dawn of the IPA was in the 19th century when it gained its world-conquering moniker.

WHAT IS IT ABOUT THESE BEERS THAT HAVE CAPTURED THE CRAFT BEER ZEITGEIST?

Beer writer and historian Martyn Cornell, who has done more than any other to explore the genesis of this particular style, has torpedoed many a myth about how IPA became so popular – uncovering the fact that beer had been shipped to the newly established Indian colonies for decades prior to the common adoption of the "India Pale Ale" name.

In fact, the majority of the British beer drinkers in India at that time preferred what they had drunk at home before they joined the East India Company – and that happened to be porter. It was the officers and gentry who (in scenes repeated throughout history) let their tastes differ from the men they commanded, and chose to drink the paler beer instead.

This "pale ale for the Indian market" was then sold into the drinking dens at home, and changed the drinking habits of a nation. Being more highly hopped meant that it lasted longer – the original intention of adding hops to beer was as a preservative rather than a flavour enhancer – so beers destined for shipping to warm climates often contained double the amount of Kentish hops.

EMBRACE THE POWER; THE POWER OF THE HOP.

As the beer morphed into "East India Pale Ale" in the mid-1830s it was well on the way to dropping the first of those words from its name and becoming a mainstay for British drinkers, whether they lived in Calcutta or Clapham. After the East India Company was wound up and Britain turned its attention elsewhere, public houses at home still continued to dispense pale ale and IPA.

Served on draft, over time these beers became lighter in body and strength, as fitted the public mood. With a toasty, bready backbone of pale ale malt, the hop levels – usually East Kent Goldings – ensured they were crisp and refreshing, but it was another adjective by which they increasingly became known, reflecting their acquired (but not soon forgotten) aftertaste – bitter.

As the alcohol levels continued to drop, bitter became the true drink of the working people of Britain. In time, it was the brewers of another old British colony that discovered the joy of the IPA: the United States of America. Here, a revolution in home-brewing in the 1970s and '80s led a nation – and then the wider world – to embrace the power of the hop.

American brewers resurrected the English-style India pale ales with the ingredients they had to hand. Instead of earthy, floral hops from Kent, they had hops from the Pacific Northwest that sang with grapefruit, orange and other citrus notes as well as sticky pine and resin. The results were transformative, and all began with a single variety – Cascade.

Anchor Brewing's Liberty Ale, released ahead of the two-hundredth anniversary of the American Revolution, was based on English pale ale, only the use of Cascade hops resulted in something very different. As Liberty hit the bars and shops in 1975, its clean and dry flavour profile won instant converts. Using whole-flower hops and then dry-hopping techniques, the San Franciscan brewery truly pioneered the style.

Even though it was referred to as American pale ale, Anchor Liberty is often held aloft as the first US craft-brewed IPA – and it was the first of many. Pale, hoppy beers lit a fire under the resurgent American brewing scene then, and have become even more seismic since. So just what is it about these beers that has captured the craft beer zeitgeist?

Well, firstly and most importantly, it's about the flavour – the tastes of beer drinkers change with every generation, and for the largest cohort today it is the citrus that leads. This then plays into the second reason – the available varieties of hops skew toward those with high levels of alpha acids, which bring bitterness and aroma in abundance. The USA, New Zealand, Australia – New World hops are it.

All hops are amazing, though, of course – the spicy noble Germanic and the earthy British hops that give blackcurrant elements to beers are no less incredible. But the market goes with the hot hand, and those from (in particular) the Yakima and Willamette valleys of the northwestern USA have the hops that craft breweries are craving. Supply and demand have always driven the IPA machine.

It's also due to familiarity. As people become more aware of beers with this flavour profile, they know what they will get when they see those three letters on a label. A random punt on a beer from time to time does everyone good (and some drinkers gravitate toward new things at every opportunity) – but IPAs are instant and accessible through this familiarity.

There's a reason that Against the Grain Brewery in Louisville, Kentucky, has a beer called simply Something Hoppy – it's what a significant proportion of their customers ask for when they wander into their brewpub. IPA has become the self-fulfilling prophecy of craft beer: more and more people are becoming educated as to the amazing flavours that it can deliver – the refreshment, the dry bitterness.

It's incredible how people's perceptions change. As this awareness increases and IPAs have become more popular, breweries have kept up with the game by adding them to their repertoire. So they appear on the shelves and bar counters more often. Here, people see them and try them, so in turn gain a taste for the resinous, the citrus and (above all) an appreciation of exactly what hops are capable of.

And with IPA, they can deliver flavour in abundance…

DEAD PONY CLUB

THE DEAD PONY SESSIONS

Second only to our flagship Punk IPA in popularity, the beer that became Dead Pony Club had its genesis in our wanting to release a beer that showcased US hops, yet at a slightly lower ABV than the range of IPAs and pale ales on the market. Not intended to run alongside Stone Pale Ale or Sierra Nevada Pale Ale, it was brewed to be a massively dry-hopped citrus bomb, at under 4% ABV.

As a result, it became a firm favourite among BrewDog fans and our brew-team almost as soon as it appeared. There are many reasons why this might be, but we figure it's most likely due to its light, aromatic and zesty flavour profile. A Californian-style session pale ale, it pays homage to the glory of the Pacific Coast, using hops from that part of the world to incredible effect.

At first sip, there's a brittle toffee malt flavour, before grapefruit and pine come crashing in – big citrus and lemongrass explode from the glass, with blossoming resinous piney flavours following soon afterward. Dead Pony Club is nothing less than a box-fresh hop hit.

This is proof – if any were needed – that you can layer flavour into beers without seeing the needle rise into the 7, 8, 9% ABV range. There's nothing wrong with that extra strength, of course, but sometimes you want the high voltages delivered with lower amplitude. When it comes to modern craft beer, you can very definitely have both. Less can always be more.

like that? try these:

SESSION IPA
11|03 MOSAIC

4.2%

Brew By Numbers, England

Massively juicy with a huge peach and apricot flavour

GO TO IPA

4.5%

Stone Brewing, USA

More caramel malt in evidence alongside a huge whack of resin

ALL DAY IPA

4.7%

Founders Brewing Co, USA

King of the modern-day American session pale ales

SESSION PALE ALE

RELEASED	2012
ABV	3.8%
STYLE	SESSION PALE ALE
IBU	40
HOPS	SIMCOE, CITRA, MOSAIC
MALT	EXTRA PALE, CARA, CRYSTAL

"DEAD PONY IS THE PERFECT SESSION BEER — IT HAS A MASSIVE KICK OF CITRUS SET AGAINST A BACKBONE OF BISCUIT MALT, AND HAS MASSES OF FLAVOUR FROM THE FRESHEST NORTH AMERICAN HOPS." — JAMES WATT

"DESPITE BEING A MASSIVE FOODIE I DIDN'T KNOW BEER WITH FLAVOUR EXISTED UNTIL I ASKED FOR 'A LAGER' IN A BREWDOG BAR. THE BARMAN SUGGESTED I TRY DPC INSTEAD. IT OPENED UP A WHOLE NEW WORLD TO ME." — EQUITY PUNK SHAUN BARNES

YOU SAY:

....
....
....
....
....
....
....

DROPTICK
TICK THIS BEER OFF YOUR LIST WITH A DROP FROM YOUR FINGER

THE STYLES

There is far more to beer than IPA of course – otherwise hop merchants would be pulling in seven-figure salaries and rolling around in Aston Martins. The guardians of the stylebook, the Beer Judge Certification Programme (BJCP), oversee an eye-watering/mouth-watering 122 different styles in their listings*, transcribed in a document 79 pages long. So where on earth do you start with that?

Well, this is usually the point in a beer book where you would dutifully read through a similar list of all the different types and commit to memory the specifics of Altbier and Zwickelbier, and everything in between. But as with everything in life, the appreciation of craft beer is a journey – one from cheapo lager, wine, cocktails or Sambuca (no judgements here), to beery nirvana. So let's help you achieve that, rather than merely getting from A to Z.

Real life consists of a series of decisions, each one opening up a path to continue onwards. So embracing that we have condensed the phone-book-sized BJCP teachings into eight different scenarios, each themed around a particular beer style. Moving forwards into three others in a progression of flavours, each in the pathway is more intriguing than the last. So if you've never tried a wheat beer, for instance, go for the first in the sequence – a Belgian Witbier.

If you already like Belgian wits, or have tried them and didn't really get it – or are reading this wearing a "Witbier 4 life" T-shirt, then start at the second or third point along the wheaty road. And if you are already familiar with each and every end-of-level-guardian in our first seven threads, we have thrown in a Wild Card route that really mixes things up. Each to his own, as they say. So let's get to it, moving away from craft beer's favourite style to the one the world drinks more of than any other...

LAGERS

FOR ANYONE WHO LIKES LAGERS BUT WONDERS IF THE GRASS IS GREENER ON THE OTHER SIDE, THE ANSWER IS A RESOUNDING YES. THE METHOD OF PRODUCING LAGERS WAS FIRST DEVELOPED IN THE 15TH CENTURY BY THE BREWING POWERHOUSES OF GERMANY. YOU DON'T THINK THEIR BEERS WOULD HAVE TASTED OF VERY LITTLE, DO YOU?

MADE WELL, LAGERS ARE A TRUE JOY. THEY ARE ALSO THE HARDEST TYPE OF BEER TO BREW. AS, FOR THE PRODUCER, THERE IS NOWHERE TO HIDE. NO MASSIVE HOP-AROMA-MASKING FAULTS. NO BARREL-AGEING TO ROUND OUT THE FLAVOURS. AND YET, THEY ARE ANYTHING BUT SIMPLE. LAGER DRINKERS, THIS PATHWAY IS YOURS. THE FOUR DIFFERENT STYLES HERE ARE YOUR ROAD TO CRAFT BEER NIRVANA. MAKE IT TO SAISON, AND YOUR LIFE WILL NOT BE THE SAME.

Lager – Kölsch – Vienna Lager – Saison

In reality, there are many different kinds of lager – but look for German Pils, the golden Helles of Munich and the myriad Pilsners of the Czech Republic. As a rule, Czech lagers are fuller and richer, whereas their German equivalents are cleaner and more bitter (Pils in particular). Brewed with classic European hops and no industrial filler, they are an excellent starting point for anyone even remotely curious about beer drinking.

ABV: 4.4–5.8%

COLOUR: 2–5°SRM (straw to pale gold)

BITTERNESS: 20–50 IBUs (pronounced; lasting)

TYPICAL INGREDIENTS: Pilsner malt, noble hops, German/Czech lager yeast

AROMAS: flowers, spice, herbs, bread

FLAVOURS: caramel, herbs, flowers, citrus, bitterness

DRINK IN THE... sun

ENJOY WITH: Brie, bruschetta, salads, pork, white fish

SERVE IN: Pilsner flute

EXAMPLES: Budweiser Budvar (Czechvar), Augustiner Lagerbier Hell, Victory Prima Pils, Weihenstephaner Original

TRIED & TASTED!

THIS DROPTICK WAS...

_____

AND I SCORED IT   /10

Lager – Kölsch – Vienna Lager – Saison

If you like a Pils (or three), then try a Kölsch. They may look similar but at heart they are fundamentally different. Although cold-conditioned they are fermented at warmer temperatures and brewed with ale yeast, they are not actually lagers. This crucial distinction results in a softer, more floral and well-rounded beer. As such, they are perfect vehicles for picking out more subtle flavours, and this pin-bright beer – made famous by the breweries of Cologne, Germany – will give you a new appreciation of the power yeast has on a beer.

ABV: 4.4–5.2%

COLOUR: 3–5°SRM (pale gold)

BITTERNESS: 18–30 IBUs (moderate; rounded)

TYPICAL INGREDIENTS: Pilsner/pale malt, German hops, ale yeast

AROMAS: subtle, bread, fruit, vinous

FLAVOURS: clean, dry, flowers, citrus, fruit

DRINK IN THE... newly mowed garden

ENJOY WITH: shellfish, pork sausage, salads, schnitzel, mild cheese

SERVE IN: Stange

EXAMPLES: Früh Kölsch, Gaffel Kölsch, Sünner Kölsch, Thornbridge Tzara

TRIED & TASTED!

THIS DROPTICK WAS...

_____

AND I SCORED IT   /10

Lager – Kölsch – **Vienna Lager** – Saison

Lagers needn't be golden. Back in the day, the increased proportion of darker malt combined with the hard, carbonate-rich waters of Central Europe produced classic beers like the amber lagers of Vienna. Their flavours are a perfect bridge between the land of the mass-produced and everything else, and although native examples are now hard to find, craft breweries have helped bring this historic style back from the brink for a new generation. Dry, crisp and hoppy, they also have a healthy dose of rich malt on the flavour: the best of all brewing worlds.

ABV: 4.7–5.5%

COLOUR: 10–15°SRM (mid-amber to copper)

BITTERNESS: 18–30 IBUs (moderate; rounded)

TYPICAL INGREDIENTS: Vienna malt, European hops, lager yeast

AROMAS: toast, bread, fruit

FLAVOURS: toast, dry, clean, bread, fruit

DRINK IN THE... Alps

ENJOY WITH: grilled tuna, chicken burgers, chilli con carne, Gruyère, pork chops

SERVE IN: Pilsner flute

EXAMPLES: Samuel Adams Boston Lager, Brooklyn Lager, Thornbridge Kill Your Darlings, Lakefront Riverwest Stein Beer

TRIED & TASTED!

THIS DROPTICK WAS...

AND I SCORED IT ___/10

Lager – Kölsch – Vienna Lager – **Saison**

The reward for making it to the end of the lager path is a whole array of aroma and flavour. Saisons were first produced for seasonal European farmworkers, and were augmented by local fruit, grains or herbs. As such they are versatile, yeast-driven and (as you'll hopefully discover) extremely tasty. If you can successfully graduate from the single-pronged bitterness of lager to embrace the myriad of flavours in the average saison – either the classic Belgian or newer hopped-up US versions – then your craft beer journey is only just beginning.

ABV: 5–7%

COLOUR: 5–10°SRM (golden-amber to orange)

BITTERNESS: 20–35 IBUs (moderate; spicy)

TYPICAL INGREDIENTS: pale malt, wheat, European hops, saison yeast

AROMAS: fruit, spice, citrus, earth, zesty

FLAVOURS: fruit, grain, pepper, lemon, dry

DRINK IN THE... long afternoons

ENJOY WITH: mussels, lobster, Taleggio cheese, chicken Caesar, Thai curry

SERVE IN: tulip glass

EXAMPLES: Saison Dupont Vieille Provision, Fantôme Saison, Brooklyn Sorachi Ace, Beavertown Quelle Saison

TRIED & TASTED!

THIS DROPTICK WAS...

AND I SCORED IT ___/10

PALE ALES

NEXT IN LINE, WE HAVE A SERIES OF STYLES BREWED WITH A BIT MORE OF EVERYTHING, AND (COMPARED TO LAGERS) CONDITIONED A LITTLE WARMER. VERY EARLY BREWERS DISCOVERED THAT IF THEY LET THEIR MALT DRY OUTSIDE, THE SUN BLEACHED IT AND THE BEER ENDED UP PALER THAN THOSE BREWED WITH THEIR REGULAR MALT. SO CENTURIES BEFORE THE SUN-DRIED TOMATO, OUR CELESTIAL LIFE-GIVER USED ITS MIGHTY RAYS TO BEGIN THE LONG HISTORY OF THE PALE ALE.

EMBRACED BY THE BRITISH IN GREAT BREWING CITIES SUCH AS BURTON UPON TRENT, DERBY, LONDON AND EDINBURGH, PALE MALT BECAME THE PERFECT CANVAS FROM WHICH TO DISPLAY THE GLORY OF THE HOP - FIRST RUSTIC ENGLISH, NOW (AS WITH EVERYTHING CRAFT) THUNDEROUS AND AMERICAN. FOR ANYONE FAMILIAR WITH GOLDEN ALES BUT LOOKING FOR MORE, THESE BEER STYLES FORM THE PERFECT EXPLORATION OF FLAVOUR.

British Golden Ale – American Pale Ale – Märzen – Belgian Tripel

This is the style to give to a beer-curious lager fan who is looking to Level Up. Pale or golden ales from the UK have more of a baseline of bitterness but are still hugely drinkable – there's a reason why they festoon the countertops of pubs up and down the country. With a dry finish lacking the sweet whack of caramel from the amber malts used in bitters, golden ales are the ultimate European session beer and a great opening to the pale ale pathway.

ABV: 3.8–5%

COLOUR: 2–5°SRM (straw to pale gold)

BITTERNESS: 20–45 IBUs (pronounced; lasting)

TYPICAL INGREDIENTS: pale malt, English or US hops, British ale yeast

AROMAS: flowers, herbs, citrus

FLAVOURS: biscuit, flowers, citrus, fruit, bitterness

DRINK IN THE... pub!

ENJOY WITH: Cheddar, pork pies, mild curries, falafel, salmon

SERVE IN: nonic pint

EXAMPLES: Hop Back Summer Lightning, Oakham JHB, Kelham Island Pale Rider, Crouch Vale Brewers Gold

British Golden Ale – American Pale Ale – Märzen – Belgian Tripel

Three words: needs more hops. Anyone who tries a British golden ale and finds that thought running through their head has truly awoken to the quintessential ingredient of craft beer. From the movement's infancy onward, the beer style that catered for that brainwave has been the APA. Long before India Pale Ale became an ever-present on US beer menus, it was the American counterpart that captured the attention of a nation. Well hopped, with a strong malt backbone, yet still easy to drink. The holy grail of brewing encapsulated in a single style.

ABV: 4.5–6.2%

COLOUR: 5–10°SRM (pale gold to gold)

BITTERNESS: 30–50 IBUs (pronounced; lasting)

TYPICAL INGREDIENTS: pale ale malt, US hops, American ale yeast

AROMAS: citrus, flowers, resin, pine, tropical

FLAVOURS: caramel, pine, citrus, stone fruit, biscuit

DRINK IN THE... summer evenings

ENJOY WITH: roast beef sandwich, double cheeseburger, apple pie, baked Camembert, fried chicken

SERVE IN: tumbler pint glass, tulip glass

EXAMPLES: Oskar Blues Dale's Pale Ale, Sierra Nevada Pale Ale, Anchor Liberty Ale, Stone Pale Ale

British Golden Ale – American Pale Ale – **Märzen** – Belgian Tripel

For the next progression we need to make a diversion back into the world of the lager. From the heartlands of European brewing comes the celebratory Märzen. Brewed in March and lagered over the summer until Germany's beer festival season, Märzens are complex and elegant, yet have a more rounded flavour than American Pale Ales due to the greater dominance of malt over hop and the higher alcohol content. Proof that although we worship the flavourful cone, it isn't the be-all and end-all of brewing – the Märzen is a true global classic.

ABV: 5.6–6.3%

COLOUR: 8–17°SRM (golden to amber)

BITTERNESS: 18–25 IBUs (medium; balanced)

TYPICAL INGREDIENTS: Pilsner/Munich malt, noble/ German hops, lager yeast

AROMAS: bread, biscuit, toast, caramel

FLAVOURS: bread, bitter, dry, sweet, clean

DRINK IN THE... Biergarten

ENJOY WITH: pork knuckle, sausage and mash, Emmental cheese, Sunday roast, pretzels

SERVE IN: Stein

EXAMPLES: Paulaner Oktoberfest, Hacker-Pschorr Oktoberfest, Left Hand Oktoberfest, Victory Festbier

British Golden Ale – American Pale Ale – Märzen – **Belgian Tripel**

Belgian Pale Ales exist – and they are fantastic – but for the end of this branch of the tree of craft beer appreciation we have to step things up a notch. So we arrive at the Belgian Tripel, a style created by the Trappist monks of the Abbey of Westmalle in response to the rise of pale ale in between World Wars I and II. Spicy, strong and aromatic, these beers deserve the utmost respect and your finest glassware – they are the pinnacle of brewing and combine each of the four main ingredients in utter harmony. Pin back your ears and go for it.

ABV: 7.5–9.5%

COLOUR: 4–7°SRM (pale gold to golden)

BITTERNESS: 20–40 IBUs (medium; balanced)

TYPICAL INGREDIENTS: Pilsner malt, European hops, Belgian ale yeast, candi sugar

AROMAS: fruit, pepper, cloves, citrus, honey

FLAVOURS: grain, sweet, spice, fruit, orange, bittersweet

DRINK IN THE... evening

ENJOY WITH: creamy pasta, lobster, duck, Gorgonzola, crème brûlée

SERVE IN: tulip glass or chalice

EXAMPLES: Westmalle Tripel, Bosteels Tripel Karmeliet, St Feuillien Tripel, Green Flash Trippel

TRIED & TASTED!

THIS DROPTICK WAS...

AND I SCORED IT   /10

TRIED & TASTED!

THIS DROPTICK WAS...

AND I SCORED IT   /10

BROWN ALES

MOVING ON, WE HAVE BEERS FOR THOSE WHO LIKE THINGS DARKER, WITH A LITTLE BITTERNESS ON THE SIDE. FOUR GLOBAL STYLES THAT BUILD ON EACH OTHER WITH SUCCESSIVE ADDITIONS OF AROMA AND FLAVOUR FROM HOPS, YEAST AND THEN MALT. WELL-MADE CASK-CONDITIONED ENGLISH BITTER IS A THING OF BEAUTY, A BEER STYLE THAT SHOULD BE (AND IS) CHERISHED. BUT FOR SOMEONE KEEN TO EXPERIMENT WITH THE VARIETY OF BEER THE WORLD CONTAINS, READ ON.

BITTER BEER CHANGED THE LANDSCAPE OF BRITISH DRINKING FROM THE MID-19TH CENTURY, REPLACING THE MILDER-TASTING ALES THAT WERE POPULAR AT THE TIME. ITS ASSOCIATION WITH PALE ALE IS LONG AND INTERTWINED, WITH THE TWO SEPARATING INTO MORE DISTINCT ENTITIES ONLY RECENTLY. THAT SAID, TRUE ENGLISH BITTER BRINGS LAYERS OF HOP-LED FLAVOUR THAT ARE THE PERFECT SPRINGBOARD FOR ANYONE WILLING TO SEE WHAT ELSE THE WORLD OF BEER HAS TO OFFER.

Bitter – American Brown Ale – Belgian Trappist Dubbel – Doppelbock

If you had to sum up bitter with a single word (in addition to the name of the style itself), then it would have to be "drinkable". Bitters are designed to be quaffed, whether from bottle or – ideally – in the pub, and are session beers without equal. In turn darker, maltier and sweeter than golden ales, bitter has been around for centuries and will hopefully still be around for many more.

ABV: 3.8–4.6%

COLOUR: 8–16°SRM (deep gold to amber)

BITTERNESS: 25–40 IBUs (medium; balanced)

TYPICAL INGREDIENTS: pale/amber/crystal malt, English hops, British ale yeast

AROMAS: bread, toast, grass, flowers, fruit

FLAVOURS: biscuit, nut, flowers, earth, bitter

DRINK IN THE... pub!

ENJOY WITH: cheese ploughman's, fish and chips, roast beef, mild curries, pork scratchings

SERVE IN: nonic pint

EXAMPLES: Fuller's London Pride, Coniston Bluebird Bitter, Harvey's Sussex Best, Anchor Small Beer

Bitter – American Brown Ale – Belgian Trappist Dubbel – Doppelbock

To progress from bitter the ideal style is the US brown ale. More a dipping of the toes than an intrepid deep dive, American browns have a rounder bitterness but offset that with a healthier lick of hops in the taste. Brewed with an increased percentage of crystal or caramel malt, they also have a higher alcohol strength, and emerged from American home-brewers putting their spin on the classic brown ales of the UK (by which we mean adding more hops). Just as drinkable as English bitter, American brown ale ups the ante in every direction.

ABV: 4.3–6.2%

COLOUR: 18–35°SRM (light brown to deep mahogany)

BITTERNESS: 20–35 IBUs (medium; balanced)

TYPICAL INGREDIENTS: pale/crystal/chocolate malt, US/NZ hops, American ale yeast

AROMAS: toast, nut, caramel, stone fruit, flowers

FLAVOURS: caramel, nut, fruit, chocolate, sweetness

DRINK IN THE... autumn

ENJOY WITH: chilli beef, grilled chicken, hoisin duck, veggie burger, chocolate soufflé

SERVE IN: nonic pint

EXAMPLES: Dogfish Head Indian Brown Ale, Sierra Nevada Tumbler, Mikkeller Jackie Brown, Brooklyn Brown Ale

Bitter – American Brown Ale – **Belgian Trappist Dubbel** – Doppelbock

Back to the monks of Europe for the next escalation, and the enveloping world of the Belgian Trappist dubbel. Originally brewed by the Trappist monasteries, they are now also created by "Abbey" breweries (which don't necessarily have to be in an abbey, but must at least be associated with one). Less rich and intense than a Tripel, they are also darker, as the malt bill is helped on its way by the addition of dark candi sugar, which aids caramelization. And if at this point you are wondering if there is such a thing as a "single", the answer is yes – it was traditionally brewed for the monks themselves.

ABV: 6–7.6%

COLOUR: 10–18°SRM (amber to brown)

BITTERNESS: 15–25 IBUs (low; balanced)

TYPICAL INGREDIENTS: Pilsner malt, European hops, candi sugar, Belgian ale yeast

AROMAS: caramel, raisins, spice, chocolate, banana

FLAVOURS: spice, dark stone fruit, caramel, cloves, raisin

DRINK IN THE... cloisters

ENJOY WITH: Edam/Gouda cheese, BBQ ribs, oxtail soup, Bavarian smoked ham, chocolate mousse

SERVE IN: tulip glass, Belgian chalice

EXAMPLES: Westmalle Trappist Dubbel, Trappistes Rochefort 6, La Trappe Dubbel, Allagash Dubbel

Bitter – American Brown Ale – Belgian Trappist Dubbel – **Doppelbock**

Topping out the bitter tree we have a beer that is anything but. We move from Trappist dubbel to Doppel with the Doppelbock, a rich, strong German lager that parries the hops of an American brown and the yeast of a Belgian Trappist dubbel by rounding everything out with centuries of Germanic brewing skill. First produced over 375 years ago in Munich (again, by monks), names ending in "-ator" are a useful spotter's guide for the style. Dopplebocks are challenging, rewarding and – in a fitting salute to the bitter – perfect examples of true balance.

ABV: 7–10%

COLOUR: 6–25°SRM (golden to dark brown)

BITTERNESS: 16–26 IBUs (low; background)

TYPICAL INGREDIENTS: Munich/Vienna/Carafa malt, noble hops, German lager yeast

AROMAS: dark fruit, chocolate, toast, toffee, alcohol

FLAVOURS: caramel, chocolate, dark fruit, rich, warming

DRINK IN THE... armchair

ENJOY WITH: venison, baked Camembert, game stews, chocolate torte, strong cheese

SERVE IN: tulip glass

EXAMPLES: Ayinger Celebrator, Tröegs Troegenator, Weihenstephaner Korbinian, Weltenburger Kloster Asam-Bock

INDIA PALE ALE

IF YOU'RE INTERESTED IN THE HISTORY OF THE IPA, DON'T LOOK TO AMERICA; TURN YOUR ATTENTION TO THE UNITED KINGDOM WHEN PUNCHING CO-ORDINATES INTO YOUR TIME MACHINE. WE'VE DISCUSSED THE HISTORY OF THE WORLD'S FAVOURITE CRAFT BEER STYLE IN DEPTH ON PAGES 78-81, BUT FOR ANYONE SEEKING A BIT MORE FROM THEIR GLASS OF LIQUID HOP JUICE, WHERE CAN THEY TURN?

WELL, THE ANSWER IS TO INCREASE THE MALT IN THE BEER AT THE SAME TIME AS RAMPING UP THE HOPS. THE INDIA PALE ALE PROGRESSION LISTED HERE IS A PERFECT MENU FOR A "VERTICAL" TASTING. PICK UP A BOTTLE OF EACH OF THE FOUR EXAMPLES AND SAMPLE THEM IN TURN. IN A VERY SHORT TIME YOU'LL DISCOVER JUST HOW THE INFLUENCE OF THE HOP IS AIDED OR TAMED BY THE INCLUSION OF HEFTIER MALT IN THE BREWING PROCESS (PLUS YOU'LL HAVE QUITE THE EVENING).

English IPA – American IPA – American Double IPA – Barley Wine

The English IPA: from the ruling classes of the Raj to you. A stronger version of English pale ale, these beers are dry where their American counterparts are punchy, and as such form the perfect entry-level IPA (which is in no way meant as a disparagement). With less malt in the brew, fewer hops are required to produce a balanced end result. For the brewer these reductions always equate to a higher level of skill to ensure an amazing beer in the end.

ABV: 5–7.5%

COLOUR: 6–14°SRM (gold to amber)

BITTERNESS: 40–60 IBUs (assertive; lasting)

TYPICAL INGREDIENTS: pale ale malt, English hops, British ale yeast. Hoorah!

AROMAS: flowers, spice, pepper, citrus, orange

FLAVOURS: citrus, grass, caramel, flowers, bread

DRINK IN THE... sunset

ENJOY WITH: prawns, medium-hot curries, mature Cheddar, mushroom stroganoff, gingerbread

SERVE IN: nonic pint

EXAMPLES: Thornbridge Jaipur, Fuller's Bengal Lancer, Brooklyn East India IPA, Harpoon IPA

English IPA – American IPA – American Double IPA – Barley Wine

As we move from one IPA to the next, the difference should be readily noticeable in the aromas and flavours. What brewers use in the USA to craft an IPA is very different from what goes into the European version: American-grown hops and malt in greater quantities. It wasn't always the case, though. As we have seen, early American IPAs were direct equivalents of their British ancestors. Over time, brewers in the USA (and increasingly, around the world) have become more generous with the hops, leading to modern hop bombs (see later).

ABV: 5.5–7.5%

COLOUR: 5–14°SRM (gold to amber)

BITTERNESS: 40–70 IBUs (aggressive; lasting)

TYPICAL INGREDIENTS: US pale malt, US hops, American ale yeast

AROMAS: citrus, pine, resin, light stone fruit, tropical fruit

FLAVOURS: citrus, resin, caramel, tropical fruit, melon

DRINK IN THE... present

ENJOY WITH: spicy salmon, Cajun burger, Thai noodles, blue cheese, cookies

SERVE IN: tumbler pint glass, tulip glass

EXAMPLES: Victory HopDevil, Stone IPA, Great Divide Titan IPA, Flying Dog Snake Dog IPA

TRIED & TASTED!

THIS DROPTICK WAS...

AND I SCORED IT   /10

TRIED & TASTED!

THIS DROPTICK WAS...

AND I SCORED IT   /10

English IPA – American IPA
– **American Double IPA** –
Barley Wine

Belgians have dubbels, Germans Doppels, so it was only natural that American brewers would eventually get in on the act and create their own doubles. They had to wait until 1994, though, when Vinnie Cilurzo of Blind Pig Brewing Company added (at least) twice of everything to his IPA recipe to test both his equipment and himself. The rest is history. Also known as imperial IPAs (a nod to the export trade of old, and also to designate the top of the tree from a stateside brewhouse), these beers are thunderous renditions of oily, punchy hops and complex, grainy maltiness. They are BIG beers.

ABV: 7.5–10%

COLOUR: 6–15°SRM (golden amber to copper)

BITTERNESS: 65–100+ IBUs (monumental; intense)

TYPICAL INGREDIENTS: US two-row/crystal malt, US hops, American ale yeast

AROMAS: resin, pine, citrus, spice, tropical fruit, alcohol

FLAVOURS: citrus, resin, pine, pith, spice, alcohol

DRINK IN THE... great outdoors

ENJOY WITH: BBQ pork, grilled lamb, blue cheese, duck terrine, carrot cake

SERVE IN: tulip glass

EXAMPLES: Stone Ruination, Dogfish Head 90 Minute IPA, Oskar Blues GUBNA, Odell Myrcenary Double IPA

English IPA – American IPA
– American Double IPA –
Barley Wine

Let's draw things to a close in your favourite armchair. The barley wine (or barleywine, either is good) is a historic but hybrid beer style encompassing the old ale, the strong ale, the vintage ale and anything else brewers pushed the boat out for. Still brewed today in the UK, Belgium and North America, they differ depending on where you pick them up – but all sit at the pinnacle of brewing. Expect your palate to be challenged, as these complex beers run at your taste buds from every possible direction (velvet drinking gown optional, but recommended).

ABV: 8–12%

COLOUR: 10–20°SRM (amber to brown)

BITTERNESS: 40–60 IBUs (assertive; lasting)

TYPICAL INGREDIENTS: caramel/pale malt, English/European/US hops, ale yeast

AROMAS: caramel, earth, sherry, spice, toffee, alcohol

FLAVOURS: caramel, vinous, toast, sherry, marmalade, molasses

DRINK IN THE... armchair

ENJOY WITH: five-spice duck, Stilton, vegetable tagine, dark chocolate, rice pudding

SERVE IN: brandy snifter

EXAMPLES: JW Lees Harvest Ale, AleSmith Old Numbskull, Anchor Old Foghorn, De Molen Bommen & Granaten

TRIED & TASTED!

THIS DROPTICK WAS...

AND I SCORED IT ___ /10

TRIED & TASTED!

THIS DROPTICK WAS...

AND I SCORED IT ___ /10

NANNY STATE

THE ORIGINAL PROTEST BEER

Nanny State was a response to the draconian Portman Group as they flailed against our recently released 18.2% ABV imperial stout Tokyo*, castigating us for "irresponsibly" brewing a beer that strong. No matter that it was a beer we loved and that we clearly stated it was to be enjoyed in small measures; our stance was not even dignified with an answer. So we vented our frustration in the only way we knew how: with another beer.

Nanny State was released at 1.1% – so low in alcohol it fell below the legal classification for beer. Emerging from our anger over the treatment of Tokyo* and some people's ignorance, the first version of Nanny State was thunderous, over 250 theoretical IBUs. With more hops than any other beer we'd created (or any other beer around at the time), it delivered a megaton of resin that really stripped the coating from your teeth.

A lot of people liked the insane, overwhelming bitterness, but in 2010 we took a step back and looked again, tweaking the recipe and dropping the IBU from 250 to 45 (and the ABV even lower, to 0.5%). As an alcohol-free beer with a more restrained bitterness it gained new purpose, over and above being a protest beer. Nanny State is now the fifth best-selling beer we make.

It's hard to brew a full-flavoured craft beer at 0.5%. But we relish tasks that aren't straightforward, and the key to Nanny State is the backbone of speciality malt laying down a base upon which the five different hops can really come to the fore. Sometimes you need to wave placards and make noise, but other times the best way to get back at people is simply to carry on doing what you do best.

like that? try these:

DRINK'IN THE SNOW

0.3%

Mikkeller, brewed at De "Proef", Belgium

A festive Drink'In the Sun – sweeter, darker and spicier

FUN

0.5%

Jever, Germany

Low-alcohol Pils with herbal and floral elements to the flavour

DRINK'IN THE SUN

0.3%

Mikkeller, brewed at De "Proef", Belgium

A refreshing, hoppy American-style wheat ale

ALCOHOL-FREE ALE

RELEASED	2009
ABV	0.5%
STYLE	IMPERIAL MILD
IBU	45
HOPS	CENTENNIAL, AMARILLO, COLUMBUS, CASCADE, SIMCOE
MALT	EIGHT DIFFERENT SPECIALITY MALTS
DRY-HOPPED	CENTENNIAL, AMARILLO

"THIS BEER IS NOT FOR THE FAINT-HEARTED – EVEN IF IT IS EFFECTIVELY ALCOHOL-FREE. ON THE PALATE THE 100% SPECIALITY MALTS WORK HARD TO BALANCE OUT THE BARRAGE OF HUMULUS LUPULUS WE THROW AT THIS BEER. THEY DO MANAGE IT, BUT NANNY STATE IS HOPPED TO THE BRINK AND BACK." — MARTIN DICKIE

"NANNY STATE IS A REAL RARITY – AN ALCOHOL-FREE BEER BREWED WITH PROPER CRAFT METHODS SO THAT IT DOESN'T FEEL OR TASTE LIKE A COMPROMISE. NO WONDER BREWDOG CAN'T BREW IT FAST ENOUGH!" — EQUITY PUNK DAVE HIGGINS

DROPTICK TICK THIS BEER OFF YOUR LIST WITH A DROP FROM YOUR FINGER

YOU SAY:

....
....
....
....
....
....

STOUTS

SO LET'S SWITCH TO THE DARK SIDE FOR A (FOUR-BEER) MINUTE. CHANCES ARE YOU KNOW SOMEONE WHO ORDERS A CERTAIN STOUT FROM A CERTAIN DUBLIN BREWERY RELIGIOUSLY ON THEIR NIGHTS OUT. FAIR ENOUGH, BUT THERE IS SO, SO, SO MUCH MORE TO DARK BEERS IN TERMS OF FLAVOUR, WITH LOTS OF THEM PACKING MORE IN THE ARSENAL THAN THAT PARTICULAR BEER. IF YOUR STOUTARIAN FRIEND WANTS TO SPREAD THEIR WINGS A LITTLE, THEN FOR STARTERS THERE'S THE CHANCE TO SLIP FROM STOUT TO PORTER.

ENTIRE BOOKS HAVE BEEN WRITTEN ABOUT THE RELATIONSHIP BETWEEN THESE TWO CLOSELY LINKED BEER STYLES, BUT ESSENTIALLY THROUGHOUT MOST OF THEIR INTERTWINED HISTORIES STOUTS WERE AKIN TO STRONG PORTERS. THAT WAS THEN, THOUGH. NOW MODERN MASS-PRODUCED STOUT HAS ENDED UP WITH A DIMINISHED FLAVOUR PROFILE, AND PARADOXICALLY TO MOVE UP IN FLAVOUR YOU REVERT TO THE WEAKER OF THE TWO BEER STYLES. SO LET'S PICK UP A PORTER...

Porter – American Porter – Scotch Ale – Imperial Stout

A beer that evolved from brown ales when advances in roasting malt created darker alternatives, British drinkers have been knocking back porter for over 300 years. It has changed a lot over that period, but modern-day releases are stunningly drinkable. Their flavours are restrained when held up alongside the other beers in this pathway, but the underlying dark roastiness is still a thing of beauty, and makes porter a great step forward from industrial stout.

ABV: 4–5.4%

COLOUR: 20–30°SRM (brown to deep brown)

BITTERNESS: 20–30 IBUs (medium; balanced)

TYPICAL INGREDIENTS: pale/brown/chocolate/roasted malt, English hops, British ale yeast

AROMAS: roasty, toast, chocolate, ash, nut

FLAVOURS: roasty, chocolate, coffee, caramel, toffee

DRINK IN THE... lunch break

ENJOY WITH: roast beef, sausage and mash, quesadillas, smoked ham, chocolate cake

SERVE IN: nonic pint

EXAMPLES: Fuller's London Porter, Harviestoun Old Engine Oil, RCH Old Slug Porter, St Peter's Old-Style Porter

Porter – American Porter – Scotch Ale – Imperial Stout

Yet another style transformed by the creativity of craft brewers – a pattern is definitely emerging – the US porter has become one of the quintessential styles for being added to. Modern versions sometimes feature coffee, chocolate, dark fruits, vanilla, cherries, salt – even bacon and maple syrup. But left unadulterated they are immensely drinkable hoppier versions of their English cousins. Too many hops and they taste very similar to black IPAs (see later), but that is the kind of discussion best left to the style geeks, and only after several beers…

ABV: 4.8–6.5%

COLOUR: 22–40°SRM (deep brown to black)

BITTERNESS: 25–50 IBUs (pronounced; lasting)

TYPICAL INGREDIENTS: black/chocolate/roasted/crystal malt, US hops, American ale yeast

AROMAS: chocolate, roasty, resin, coffee, toffee

FLAVOURS: roasty, chocolate, resin, burnt sugar, citrus

DRINK IN THE... backwoods

ENJOY WITH: smoked brisket, grilled lamb, steak pies, Cheddar, tiramisu

SERVE IN: tumbler pint glass

EXAMPLES: Anchor Porter, Sierra Nevada Porter, Deschutes Black Butte Porter, Odell Cutthroat Porter

TRIED & TASTED!

THIS DROPTICK WAS…

AND I SCORED IT   /10

TRIED & TASTED!

THIS DROPTICK WAS…

AND I SCORED IT   /10

Porter – American Porter – **Scotch Ale** – Imperial Stout

For the third beer in this dark quartet we move back from America and detour north of Hadrian's Wall. The Scotch ale – also known as the Wee Heavy – is maltier than either that have gone before, and is like drinking a liquid dessert. That said, it should never be cloyingly sweet, just give a suggestion of warmth and chewiness. Often brewed for export, Scotch ales reflect the wild and rugged nature of their homeland by countering the cold with that boozy – sometimes slightly smoky – flavour profile. They are the beery equivalent of a thermos in the rucksack.

ABV: 6.5–10%

COLOUR: 15–25°SRM (brown to deep ruby brown)

BITTERNESS: 20–35 IBUs (medium; balanced)

TYPICAL INGREDIENTS: pale malt, roasted barley, English hops, Scottish ale yeast

AROMAS: caramel, roasty, toffee, smoke, alcohol

FLAVOURS: caramel, dark stone fruit, toffee, alcohol, peat

DRINK IN THE... Highlands

ENJOY WITH: game birds, haggis, smoked salmon, sausages, sticky toffee pudding

SERVE IN: brandy snifter or thistle glass

EXAMPLES: Orkney Skullsplitter, Traquair House Jacobite Ale, Oskar Blues Old Chub, AleSmith Wee Heavy

Porter – American Porter – Scotch Ale – **Imperial Stout**

If you want an end-of-level guardian to defeat in order to claim your dark beer prize, then all roads lead to the nearest imperial stout. These are intense, epic re-imaginings of thick, dark beers exported to the imperial courts of Russia from the English family brewers of old. Tar-like and pitch black, for bonus points – and a drinking experience like no other – seek out a barrel-aged version, where the aromas and flavours listed below will be buttressed by a soft vanilla and oaky finish that (in the best examples) verges on the truly spectacular.

ABV: 8–12%

COLOUR: 30–40°SRM (very deep brown to black)

BITTERNESS: 50–90 IBUs (assertive; lasting)

TYPICAL INGREDIENTS: pale, roasted, chocolate or black malt, US hops, American ale yeast

AROMAS: roasty, coffee, chocolate, dark fruit, tobacco, alcohol

FLAVOURS: chocolate, cocoa, coffee, molasses, roasty, dark stone fruit, alcohol

DRINK IN THE... dark

ENJOY WITH: steak, Gorgonzola, mac & cheese, vanilla ice cream, chocolate truffles

SERVE IN: brandy snifter

EXAMPLES: Great Divide Yeti, AleSmith Speedway Stout, Dieu du Ciel! Péché Mortel, Magic Rock Bearded Lady

TRIED & TASTED!

THIS DROPTICK WAS...

AND I SCORED IT ____ /10

TRIED & TASTED!

THIS DROPTICK WAS...

AND I SCORED IT ____ /10

WHEAT BEERS

MORE THAN ANY OTHER STYLE ASIDE FROM LAGER, WHEAT BEER HAS FALLEN VICTIM TO THE INDUSTRIAL BREWERS. WHETHER BUYING OUT MUCH-LOVED HISTORICAL PRODUCERS OR UNABASHEDLY LAUNCHING THEIR OWN FAUX-CRAFT VERSIONS, THERE ARE A LOT OUT THERE THAT CAN LEAD YOU AWAY FROM BEERS BREWED WITH INTEGRITY, PASSION AND COMMITMENT. AND THAT IS A HUGE PITY, BECAUSE WHEAT BEERS ARE ONE OF THE TRUE GLOBAL STYLES, WITH ENORMOUS VARIETY.

TAKE OUR FABULOUS FOURSOME HERE. ONE BELGIAN AND THREE GERMAN, THESE BEERS ARE ALL HUGELY DISTINCTIVE AND REFLECT THE DIVERSITY YOU CAN DISCOVER IN BEERS THAT DIFFER ONLY IN BEING BREWED IN DIFFERENT REGIONS OF THE WORLD. THESE ARE HISTORIC STYLES WITH PEDIGREES HUNDREDS OF YEARS OLD – THE ORIGINAL "WHITE" ALES (WIT-AND-WEISS REFLECT THAT COLORATION) CAN TRACE THEIR LINEAGE BACK TO MEDIEVAL TIMES. CAN THE NEW FAKERS SAY THAT? NO. THEY CAN'T.

Belgian Witbier – Dunkleweiss – Gose – Weizenbock

Many beers have been brought back from the dead (there are at least two in this pathway), but the Belgian Wit has one of the best stories of all. Resurrected in a Belgian hayloft by a former milkman called Pierre Celis, the style that had died in 1955 with the last brewery closure was reborn ten years later with Hoegaarden. What happened to Pierre is by turns inspirational and heart-breaking (involving a fire, emigration and two separate takeovers), but although the beer he created is a shadow of its former self, his legacy is the hundreds of examples we can all now enjoy drinking.

ABV: 4.5–5.5%

COLOUR: 2–4°SRM (pale straw to pale gold)

BITTERNESS: 8–20 IBUs (low; creamy)

TYPICAL INGREDIENTS: pale malt, wheat (usually 50/50), European hops, coriander, citrus peel, Belgian ale yeast

AROMAS: spice, citrus, grain, herbal, pepper

FLAVOURS: bread, spice, pith, citrus, herbal, vanilla

DRINK IN THE... sunshine

ENJOY WITH: feta cheese, mussels, chicken salad, sashimi, vanilla panna cotta

SERVE IN: tulip glass

EXAMPLES: Brasserie du Bocq Blanche de Namur, Stone Citrusy Wit, Einstök Icelandic White Ale, Allagash White

Belgian Witbier – Dunkleweiss – Gose – Weizenbock

In deepest Bavaria, there exists a series of spellbinding dark wheat beers: the Dunkleweiss. It is a secret that has long since escaped the pine-clad mountains; now brewers around the world add roasted malt to their wheat beer recipes to produce these masterly beers. Also known as Dunkelweizen (particularly in the USA), they add another facet for the lover of the witbier – the complex interplay of darker malts. Highly carbonated, they are just as refreshing as their paler cousins and are proof that a slight twist to the malt bill can deliver amazing results.

ABV: 4.3–5.6%

COLOUR: 14–23°SRM (deep amber to brown)

BITTERNESS: 10–18 IBUs (low; reserved)

TYPICAL INGREDIENTS: Munich/Vienna malt, wheat (at least 50/50), noble hops, Weizen ale yeast

AROMAS: roasty, bread, banana, cloves, spice, bubble gum

FLAVOURS: banana, cloves, grain, caramel, bread

DRINK IN THE... Black Forest

ENJOY WITH: roast chicken, mild curries, pork knuckle, Parmesan crisps, banana bread

SERVE IN: Weizen vase

EXAMPLES: Weihenstephaner Hefeweissbier Dunkel, Ayinger Ur-Weisse, Erdinger Weissbier Dunkel, Samuel Adams Dunkelweizen

TRIED & TASTED!

THIS DROPTICK WAS...

AND I SCORED IT   /10

TRIED & TASTED!

THIS DROPTICK WAS...

AND I SCORED IT   /10

Belgian Witbier – Dunkleweiss – Gose – Weizenbock

Staying in the same country, but moving up several gears, we have a style that was born in the Middle Ages, peaked at the turn of the 20th century and was then wiped out by war and apathy. Now rediscovered in its native Germany and embraced by craft breweries, the Gose is truly unique. Highly carbonated, fruity and at the same time very tart, this wheat beer is brewed with added coriander and salt to leave a flavour unlike any other. It may be a struggle at first, but if you've ever eaten salted chocolate you'll know how it can lift flavours to new levels.

ABV: 4–5%

COLOUR: 3–4°SRM (pale straw to pale gold)

BITTERNESS: 5–10 IBUs (very low; muted)

TYPICAL INGREDIENTS: wheat, Pilsner malt, German hops, coriander seeds, salt, Weizen ale yeast, lactobacillus

AROMAS: herbs, sharp, tart, fruit, bread

FLAVOURS: bread, lemon, salt, tart, herbs, dry

DRINK IN THE... dunes

ENJOY WITH: citrus-dressed salads, scallops, white fish, thick-cut ham, Taleggio cheese

SERVE IN: tulip glass

EXAMPLES: Bayerischer Bahnhof Leipziger Gose, Westbrook Gose, Magic Rock Salty Kiss, To Øl Gose to Hollywood

Belgian Witbier – Dunkleweiss – Gose – Weizenbock

And then we arrive at the Weizenbock. Anything ending in those four letters guarantees you a strong, flavourful beer and the deep, dark, fortifying wheat beers of Bavaria are the perfect finishing point for anyone interested in this particular grain. First developed in the early years of the 20th century, there are two distinct branches – the lighter versions and the darker. Both are a meal in a glass, and our advice is to find one of each hue and sample them side by side to discover which you prefer. Maybe book the next day off work first, though.

ABV: 6.5–9%

COLOUR: 6–25°SRM (pale gold to deep brown)

BITTERNESS: 15–30 IBUs (medium; balanced)

TYPICAL INGREDIENTS: Pilsner/Munich/Vienna malt, wheat, German hops, Weizen ale yeast

AROMAS: bread, cloves, vanilla, dark stone fruit, banana, alcohol

FLAVOURS: stone fruit, cloves, bread, sherry, banana, chocolate

DRINK IN THE... winter

ENJOY WITH: pork and dumplings, roast chicken, Brunswick ham, hard cheeses, banana split

SERVE IN: tulip glass

EXAMPLES: Schneider Aventinus (Dark), Weihenstephaner Vitus (Light), Unertl Weissbier Bock (Dark), Victory Moonglow (Dark)

TRIED & TASTED!

THIS DROPTICK WAS...

AND I SCORED IT   /10

SOURS

WE NEED TO TALK ABOUT SOURS. THE UMBRELLA STYLE MOST LIKELY TO PUT SOMEONE OFF WITH A SINGLE SIP, THEY ARE HUGELY REWARDING FOR THOSE WHO CAN GET PAST THE INITIAL SHOCK. JUST AS LEMONS, SAUERKRAUT, PICKLES AND WORCESTER SAUCE CRINKLE UP THE FACE, SO DO THESE BEERS THAT BEGAN LIFE IN THE GREAT BREWING REGIONS OF CONTINENTAL EUROPE. AND JUST LIKE THOSE FOODS, ONCE YOU GAIN A TASTE FOR THEM THEY CAN TAKE OVER YOUR LIFE – THERE'S NO GOING BACK.

IT'S LITTLE USE ATTEMPTING TO BREAK YOUR SOUR VIRGINITY WITH A LAMBIC – YOU'LL PROBABLY NEVER GO NEAR THEM AGAIN (UNLESS YOU LIKE THEM RIGHT OFF THE BAT, IN WHICH CASE ALL CREDIT TO YOU). THE BEST WAY IS TO BUILD UP SLOWLY THROUGH THE LEVELS OF TARTNESS UNTIL YOU CAN FULLY APPRECIATE THE GLASSES OF AIRBORNE MAGIC FROM THE FARMLANDS OUTSIDE BRUSSELS. AS WITH MANY OTHER CHALLENGING FOODS OR DRINKS, THE FIRST STEP IS TO SEEK OUT A VERSION TEMPERED WITH JUICY, MOREISH FRUIT...

Kriek – Berliner Weisse – Flanders Red – Lambic

Alongside its close cousins the Framboise and the Cassis (raspberries and blackcurrants respectively), the Kriek is a fruit-infused lambic that tempers the sourness with a blast of fruit (in this case cherries). There's no involved, complicated brewhouse procedures for this – as often as not the brewers simply dump buckets of cherries into a fermenting barrel of lambic and leave them to get on with it. You'll be very glad they did.

ABV: 5–7%

COLOUR: 15–20°SRM (deep amber to red)

BITTERNESS: 10–20 IBUs (medium; restrained)

TYPICAL INGREDIENTS: Pilsner malt, wheat, European hops, cherries, wild yeast

AROMAS: cherry, earth, hay, oak

FLAVOURS: cherry, tart, sour, vanilla, dry

DRINK IN THE... early evening (as an apéritif)

ENJOY WITH: dark chocolate, goats' cheese, duck, Belgian waffles, pâté

SERVE IN: tulip glass

EXAMPLES: Cantillon Kriek, Lindemans Kriek, Boon Kriek, New Belgium Transatlantique Kriek

Kriek – Berliner Weisse – Flanders Red – Lambic

Next up we have another regional speciality that has flourished as craft brewers have spread their collective wings. The characteristic wheat beers of Berlin are very pale, highly carbonated and seriously sour. Yet it's a clean, refreshing sourness compared to lambic; the beers are enormously drinkable – even more so when they have fruit or fruit syrup added, as they almost always do in their homeland. Instead of the artificial syrup – either red, *ein Rotes*, or green, *ein Grünes* – many craft-brewed Berliner Weisse have fruit included in the recipe; you'll rarely find them *ohne Schuss* (without syrup).

ABV: 2.8–3.8%

COLOUR: 2–3°SRM (pale straw)

BITTERNESS: 3–5 IBUs (ultra low; barely evident)

TYPICAL INGREDIENTS: wheat, Pilsner malt, German yeast, lactobacillus, brettanomyces

AROMAS: sour, tart, lemon, apple, dough, yoghurt

FLAVOURS: lactic, tart, lemon, fruit (if syrup or fruit added)

DRINK IN THE... pavement café

ENJOY WITH: green salad, poached fish, Edam/Gouda cheese, pretzels, cheesecake

SERVE IN: goblet

EXAMPLES: Bayerischer Bahnhof Berliner Weisse, Dogfish Head Festina Pêche, J Wakefield Dragon Fruit Passion Fruit Berliner, Siren Calypso

Kriek — Berliner Weisse — `Flanders Red` — Lambic

It's back to Belgium for the next round, as unlike the first two beers our next progression rarely has anything added to it — and when you taste it, you'll see why. Our early inspiration Michael Jackson referred to the Flanders Reds as the "Burgundies of Belgium" due to their deep red hue and two years of ageing in oaken barrels. During that time they take on astonishing character from a range of wild and naturally occurring yeasts and bacteria, which might not sound pleasant, but as your appreciation of sours evolves, you'll realize they elevate barrel-ageing to an art form.

ABV: 4.5–6.5%

COLOUR: 10–15°SRM (dark amber to brown)

BITTERNESS: 10–25 IBUs (moderate; restrained)

TYPICAL INGREDIENTS: Vienna/Munich/cara malt, maize, European hops, wild yeast/bacteria

AROMAS: tart, sour, fruit, berries, oak

FLAVOURS: fruit, sour, vinous, tart, berries, acid

DRINK IN THE... deckchair

ENJOY WITH: beef stew, mussels, sharp Cheddar, grilled beef, cherry cake

SERVE IN: tulip glass

EXAMPLES: Rodenbach Grand Cru, Verhaeghe Duchesse De Bourgogne, Rodenbach Caractère Rouge, The Bruery Oude Tart

Kriek — Berliner Weisse — Flanders Red — `Lambic`

You could argue that all beery paths lead here, not just the sours. Lambic is the world's most challenging, unique and storied beer style — it's as simple as that. Ancient, masterfully brewed and blended (look for gueuzes: they are lambics of different ages blended together), these beers are left to ferment spontaneously by allowing wild yeast to fall into open tanks at night. They are miracles of beermaking, and result in a drink that is likely to have you recoiling at first. But please, please persist — eventually something will click and your beer-drinking life will not be the same again.

ABV: 5–8%

COLOUR: 3–10°SRM (pale straw to golden)

BITTERNESS: 0–10 IBUs (very low; restrained)

TYPICAL INGREDIENTS: wheat, Pilsner malt, European hops, wild yeast/bacteria

AROMAS: sour, hay, leather, citrus, apple, horse, oak

FLAVOURS: sour, lactic, rhubarb, sharp apple, crisp, tart

DRINK IN THE... hot sun

ENJOY WITH: crab, smoked salmon mousse, Gorgonzola, sticky toffee pudding, chocolate fondant

SERVE IN: tulip glass

EXAMPLES: Cantillon Geuze, Lindemans Geuze Cuvée René, Boon Oude Geuze Mariage Parfait, Drie Fonteinen Oud Geuze

WILD CARDS

OK, YOU'VE MADE IT TO THE FINAL FOUR. THESE BEERS HAVE BEEN INCLUDED AS WILD CARDS BECAUSE THEY EXIST TO CHALLENGE PERCEPTIONS OF THE WORLD'S FAVOURITE BEVERAGE – AND AS YOU'VE WORKED YOUR WAY THROUGH THE PATHWAYS BEFOREHAND (OR JUST SKIPPED TO THE END), THIS IS THE FINAL TEST. CAN AN INDIA PALE ALE BE BLACK? SHOULD BEER TASTE OF BACON? WHAT HAPPENS WHEN YOU FREEZE BEER DURING THE BREWING PROCESS? AND WHY THE HELL IS INDUSTRIAL LAGER IN THERE?

THE ANSWERS TO THESE QUESTIONS ARE TO BE FOUND ON THE FOLLOWING PAGES, AND IN YOUR GLASSWARE. BUT TO ACT AS A SPOILER THEY ARE EXCITING THINGS AND SHOW HOW FAR YOU'VE COME. THIS BOOK EXISTS TO SHOWCASE THE STUNNING VARIETY OF CRAFT BEER. WHAT BETTER CONTROL STYLE THAN THE BEER THAT STILL DOMINATES THE WORLD? ANYWAY, LET'S BEGIN THE FINISHING LAP WITH A BEER THAT BALANCES THE TWIN PILLARS OF BREWING – MALT AND HOPS.

Black IPA – Rauchbier – Eisbock – Industrial Lager

A beer of the Noughties, Black IPA surged in popularity after the Y2K bug had faded into the rear-view mirror. An IPA with a changed-up malt bill, the style is a quintessential example of the can't-leave-it-alone creativity of craft brewers. Born of the land where the hop is king – the Pacific Northwest of the United States – the addition of darker malt into the brew gives a complementary roasty note that really helps the IPA flavours sing. If you're lucky, on tasting you'll pinpoint the exact moment of transition when one gives way to the other (usually citrus into roast).

ABV: 5.5–9%

COLOUR: 25–40°SRM (deep brown to black)

BITTERNESS: 50–90 IBUs (assertive; lasting)

TYPICAL INGREDIENTS: pale/roast malts, US hops, American ale yeast

AROMAS: citrus, resin, pine, tropical fruit, chocolate

FLAVOURS: citrus, resin, pine, roasty, chocolate

DRINK IN THE... taproom

ENJOY WITH: beef tacos, pork belly, blue cheese, falafel burger, chocolate torte

SERVE IN: tumbler pint glass

EXAMPLES: Firestone Walker Wookey Jack, 21st Amendment Back in Black, Buxton Imperial Black, Beavertown Black Betty

Black IPA – Rauchbier – Eisbock – Industrial Lager

So we mentioned that lambic is the world's most acquired taste – but as with everything beery, whatever Belgium can provide there's an alternative over the border in Germany. Ditto history, as this particular style is one of the earliest around – before kilned malt, the grains were darkened over beechwood fires, and the smoky malt carried its flavour to the end product. Literally "smoke beers", these centre around the town of Bamberg in the German region of Upper Franconia, and are immense, iconic and – thanks to the new prevalence of smoked "Rauchmalz" – available in ever-increasing numbers.

ABV: 5–6%

COLOUR: 12–20°SRM (amber to brown)

BITTERNESS: 20–30 IBUs (medium; restrained)

TYPICAL INGREDIENTS: Munich/Rauch malt, German hops, German lager yeast

AROMAS: wood, smoke, bacon, toast

FLAVOURS: bacon, wood, smoke, herbs, toast

DRINK IN THE... campsite

ENJOY WITH: roast pork, griddled salmon, cured ham, sausages, ginger cake

SERVE IN: stein

EXAMPLES: Aecht Schlenkerla Rauchbier Märzen, Eisenbahn Rauchbier, Kaiserdom Rauchbier, Stone Smoked Porter

TRIED & TASTED!

THIS DROPTICK WAS...

AND I SCORED IT   /10

TRIED & TASTED!

THIS DROPTICK WAS...

AND I SCORED IT   /10

Black IPA – Rauchbier – **Eisbock** – Industrial Lager

Put food in the freezer and it'll lock in the flavours. Put beer in, and its flavours will be concentrated. Alcohol has a lower freezing point than water, so brewers can remove the ice in stages, each time making the surviving beer stronger – and at the same time enhancing the roasty, sweet and fruity flavours. Eisbocks began life in northern Bavaria but broke free in an ABV arms race that took place in the early 2010s. We may have had something to do with that. Anyway, there isn't a more perfect fireside sipper; these beers are truly, truly enormous.

ABV: 9–45%+

COLOUR: 18–30°SRM (dark amber to brown)

BITTERNESS: 25–35 IBUs (medium; balanced)

TYPICAL INGREDIENTS: Pilsner/Munich/Vienna/Carafa malt, noble hops, German lager yeast, Champagne yeast

AROMAS: sherry, dark fruit, stone fruit, leather, toffee, caramel

FLAVOURS: sherry, port, caramel, dark stone fruit, chocolate, alcohol

DRINK IN THE... deepest midwinter

ENJOY WITH: smoked duck, venison, baked Camembert, chocolate fondant, plum pudding

SERVE IN: Brandy Snifter

EXAMPLES: Kulmbacher Eisbock, Schneider Aventinus Weizen-Eisbock, De Struise Black Magic, De Molen Epitaph

Black IPA – Rauchbier – Eisbock – **Industrial Lager**

Here we are. Head to your nearest supermarket or corner shop and stock up on whatever stands out the most from the lager aisle. Chill in the fridge to near-Eisbock levels of coldness and chug the cap off. Pour the beer into a large, cold pint glass and take in the aromas. Hmm. OK, have a sip and revel in the...ah, forget it. These lagers have a place, but hopefully it is not one that you still inhabit, because there's a whole world of other options out there waiting...

ABV: 4.2–5.3%

COLOUR: 2–4°SRM (pale straw to straw)

BITTERNESS: 8–15 IBUs (low; controlled)

TYPICAL INGREDIENTS: US six-row/two-row malt, rice, corn, US hops, American lager yeast

AROMAS: grain, sweet, corn

FLAVOURS: corn, biscuits, grain, floral

DRINK IN THE... past

ENJOY WITH: mild cheese, corn on the cob, chips, light Mexican food, pretzels

SERVE IN: the bottle (or tumbler pint glass)

EXAMPLES: Turn on the television...

DIY DOG

HOW TO HOME-BREW

Re-creating the work of others is something that we do far more than we realize. Every time we open a recipe book, for instance, it's to replicate the labours of a particular chef. It goes beyond the basic desire to eat; cookbooks exist to give us a chance to feel in tune with a person whose style we like. It's not just food, of course – every time we pull out our favourite tattered football shirt, or flick on Whitney Houston and reach for the hairbrush, we are consciously reinventing the work of someone else.

And it is just the same with home-brew.

At least, it is today. Back throughout history, you didn't roll up your sleeves on a Saturday morning to deliberately copy the output of your favoured craft brewery – it was to satisfy a more fundamental need. If a household wanted beer, they had to make it themselves. From Mesopotamians to Romans to the alewives of medieval Europe, brewing your own was part of the general routine of life. When the alternatives were wine or strange-smelling water, a batch of beer containing boiled water was a much safer, easier-to-come-by option.

For centuries this continued to be the case. The great estates of Europe had breweries in outbuildings to keep the beer cellars stocked. Those who could added vineyards, but beer required less in the way of high-intensity ingredients, so made more sense in the short term. Strong beers from the first runnings of the wort were followed by weaker brews produced with what remained, with the resultant "table beer" becoming a staple for all members of the household (down to the surprisingly young).

That's just how brewing was – it was all home-brew. There were commercial breweries back then, of course, but the industry we know today didn't begin appearing until a series of industrial revolution-era breakthroughs enlarged their economies of scale. Eureka moments such as the drum roaster for malt, the hydrometer, the discovery of what yeast actually was and the concept of refrigeration meant that brewing could become a business. Beer grew up and moved out of the home.

But people still brewed their own, irrespective of the greater availability of beer in their day-to-day lives – and they continue to do so today, in ever-increasing numbers. It has moved away from being a necessity and become simply a hobby, but why do people continue to create their own beers rather than pick them up from a shop or online?

To answer, let's play a quick game of "Why We Home-brew"…

1. TO SATISFY CURIOSITY

Sometimes you have an itch that you just can't scratch. Tasting the beer is all well and good – and you can read a brewery blog or well-intended craft beer book (tell your friends), or even visit a brewery and pin the head brewer to the wall to ask questions. But in reality the only way to discover how beer is made, what fermentation is and whether you can add nine different types of chilli to a beer and still produce something drinkable is to have a go yourself. You can answer any questions you set yourself, any self-issued challenge, through home-brewing.

The beauty of it is that it's real brewing, downsized into a microcosm of the daily routines we at BrewDog and every other craft brewer go through every time we pull up the shutters in the morning. Yet with some crucial differences. You can brew whatever you like, whenever you like (we have orders to think about), and if you make a mess of things, it doesn't really matter. If we forget to clean a tank before using it, the consequences don't bear thinking about. But you can (and should) go ahead and scratch that itch.

2. TO EVENTUALLY GO PRO

By no means the end game for every garage superhero, but the amazing grounding that home-brewing gives has been the introduction to a profession for many of the most highly regarded brewers in the world. Because the thing is, once you have mastered the basic processes and principles, it really isn't that complex. Sure, you can then add all kinds of ingredients and move on to fascinating styles – but the nuts and bolts of home-brewing follow through to every other kind of beer making.

If you want to learn more about the majesty of beer, then it is the perfect hobby. The only danger is that once you've spent many months working on hitting your gravities exactly, and discovering precisely how much Rauchmalt to add to your smoke beer, sitting at the desk on Monday morning becomes less and less appealing. Pretty soon you're formulating recipes on your PC, printing things off on the sly and finding yourself gazing out of the window thinking about Cascade hops. If you grow a beard, you're done for.

3. TO JOIN A COMMUNITY

The old saying has it that "beer people are good people" and this is very much our experience. And that sentiment applies to the amateurs as well as the professionals. More so than in any other aspect of the beer industry, the disparate people around the world who create their own beers in their kitchens or wherever can come together online (or in person) for advice. Got a stuck mash? Find a forum. Need tasting notes on your imperial blueberry Weizenbock? Take it to a home-brewers' meet-up.

You will get serious, knowledgeable feedback because if you've succumbed to an off-flavour (in your beer, that is), then chances are someone else will have been there before and can help out. This is the real positive of critiquing the work of others: it raises their game and makes them more likely to want to ask questions in the future. Plus meetings of home-brewers always – always – have beer. So there's that.

4. TO RE-CREATE YOUR FAVOURITES

Sure, you can throw caution to the wind and experiment with 40 different ingredients – you have the total freedom of the home-brew mash tun – but to truly test yourself the great thing about home-brewing is that you can try to re-create a beer you know and love and see how close you come. Take our recipes, starting on page 145. Have a crack at whichever takes your fancy and then, once it's bottled and ready to go (or kegged if you are really flash), taste alongside the real McCoy and see.

The depth of appreciation you can gain from replicating something you've been drinking for years is amazing. You'll also find it will totally change the way you see, discuss, smell and taste beer in the future. Every beer you drink becomes something to be analyzed, dissected and, potentially, re-created. If you sample something a pro has done and find fault with it, it will make you sit up on your bar stool a little straighter. Honing your skills in your kitchen or garage becomes inspiring.

...AND WHILE WE'RE ON THE SUBJECT, HERE'S WHY PEOPLE DON'T HOME-BREW...

1. TO MAKE BEER CHEAPLY

This is a total fallacy – maybe back in the day it was the case, with kits containing concentrated beer syrup that were sold in pharmacies. Making your own beer for a few pennies a pint may have been an option then, but these days the prices of different pieces of kit, additions, small packets of hops and malt – it all adds up. Plenty of people start off with the dream of cheap beer and have it dashed by their credit card statement. Home-brewers are curious and committed – but they aren't cheapskates.

THE KIT
WHAT YOU NEED TO BECOME A DIY DOG

The beauty of home-brewing is that it can be as simple as you like. All you need is something in which to boil, a few sturdy plastic containers, a thermometer and somewhere for the brewed beer (bottles and capper are easiest). Oh, and the most important thing of all – a sanitizer.

The continued beauty of home-brewing is that you can then add to this set-up with as many bells and whistles as you like – from more buckets to stainless over plastic to temperature-controlling systems that wouldn't be out of place in your local microbrewery. These can be added when the bug bites, increasing your pull on this new hobby as well as improving the quality and yield of the beer you produce.

As we'll see later, there are different grades of home-brewing, from extract through to all-grain – and although many people start with the former, it's not that difficult to amass the basic equipment needed to try genuine, brewing-with-malted-grains beer making.

So with that intention in mind, here's what you'll need…

A MASH TUN

Extract brewing (see page 124) begins with heating up pre-mixed syrup, so if you're starting via this route you'll only need a mash tun when you start all-grain brewing.

For all-grain brewing everything starts with the mash, so for this you'll need a large plastic bucket with a tap at the base and a false bottom for filtration. The trick is

successfully regulating the temperature of the mash, so one way to help lower variation is to use a cool box instead – the thick walls work really well for the opposite aim; keeping your mash warm.

Advanced option: Some top-of-the-range home-brew mash vessels have filters included rather than the false bottom (i.e. a fitted filter rather than a removable base). As you're all about efficiency, a bespoke filter may well be worth the initial outlay.

A BREWING POT

You'll also need a large, sturdy pan. You can boil on your stovetop, so find the largest cooking pot you can – remember to check that it fits under your extractor fan, leaving room for you to add things and stir. Large-scale kitchen pots are the best, like the ones used to cook lobsters or industrial quantities of potatoes for school dinners. Anything around 22-litre (6-gallon) is good.

Advanced option: Having an electric boiler means you can take your brews out of the kitchen and into the garage, say, or somewhere else you might not get in the way as much. Thermostat-controlled, these heat up using internal elements, plus they often have an outlet tap built in to remove the wort.

TWO PLASTIC BUCKETS

Once the hot side of the brewing process is complete, you'll need somewhere for the beer to ferment and then somewhere else for it to condition. A couple of 30-litre (8-gallon) heavy-duty plastic containers, etched with a scale for working out quantities, are fine for this. You can transfer from the fermentation bucket into a conditioning bucket, or into a bucket with a bottling wand fitted and dissolved priming sugar inside, so your beer can go straight into bottles (more on which later).

Advanced option: Glass carboys are more interesting to look at than an anonymous plastic bucket, as you can see what's going on inside. Alternatively, you can go a step further and use stainless steel – or even buy small-scale brewery-style fermentation vessels for your garage.

WORT CHILLER

Some home-brewers think this is an advanced option in itself – and it's true, you don't need a specifically made device to cool the wort before transfer and pitching take place. The liquid will reduce in temperature as soon as you turn off the stove and stop the boil. But a coil of copper that allows cold water to run inside will cool your wort from boiling to a required temperature in minutes rather than hours, so it really is worth the investment.

Advanced option: Flat plate chillers, with a bigger surface area and gravity doing the work, give a much quicker rate of temperature decrease (and you can buy them with increasing numbers of plates). Of course, this comes at a cost. But then, doesn't everything?

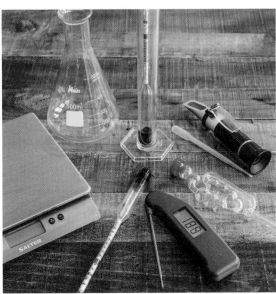

AIRLOCK

As you hopefully realize by now, when beer ferments the yeasts produce carbon dioxide and, if you let that happen in a tightly sealed plastic bucket, eventually you'll have a beer-flavoured grenade situation. Airlocks are vital home-brew equipment: plugged into the plastic lid of the fermentation bucket they let the bubbles of CO_2 bleed out of your developing beer while preventing oxygen from getting in – and, most importantly of all, stopping any beery explosions from ruining your carpet.

Advanced option: Plastic or rubber airlocks can be found for loose change. If your beer is on the vigorous side you could use a blow-off tube instead, and let the pressure bubble out through a separate bucket of sanitizer rather than block your airlock.

MEASURING DEVICES

You need to be precise with brewing – throw in too much malt, or fail to boil vigorously enough, and the beer won't pass the taste test. Plus you need a hydrometer, or you might as well just forget about it and read a book. So add to your order a dependable set of scales, a thermometer, a hydrometer and accompanying measuring jar, and a couple of lined measuring jugs.

Advanced option: You can pay all kinds of money for electronic scales, infrared thermometers or crystal measuring jugs hand-blown by Italian craftsmen – but as long as what you buy is sturdy and consistent, go with whatever is the most comfortable and hard-wearing. (Save your money and invest in a better boiler).

CLEANING SOLUTIONS

Professional brewers are clean freaks, and home-brewers should be, too. Any piece of equipment that comes into contact with wort or beer should be washed and sanitized before being used again, to prevent bacterial infection and wild yeast from ruining your entire batch (and batches to come). Invest in an antibacterial cleaning agent and a disinfecting sanitizer (such as iodophor or StarSans) – and use them both, every time.

Advanced option: There's really no need to scrimp here, the potential results just aren't worth it. You can sanitize with bleach instead of a brand-name disinfectant (1 tablespoon per 4.5 litres/1 gallon, steep for 20 minutes), but you're just as well buying the real deal. Also invest in some plastic scrubbing brushes – not wire ones as scratches can harbour bacteria.

BOTTLES & CAPS

Chances are you have a ready-to-go supply of bottles nestling in your recycling bin – so make like a true home-brewer and start hoarding those empties. You can buy empty glass bottles, but when there are so many out there already filled with craft beer, you may as well get double the enjoyment out of each one. You will need to purchase new caps and a crown-capping machine; hand cappers are pretty cheap, though, and a great way to work on the guns while finishing off a brew-day.

Advanced option: The pro alternative is to keg your beers; for this you'll obviously need some kegs (small Doliums® or Cornelius kegs are best) and a gas supply, plus a way of filling and emptying. You could cask your beer, if you are truly expert, and scan the classifieds for first-fill whisky barrels for your garage…

INGREDIENTS

Let's face it, these are the most interesting things to purchase when you're about to start making your own beer. The malt, hops and yeast can take your adventures in dozens of different directions, from the classic lagers of continental Europe to the powerhouse IPAs of the USA. Plus you can add anything to your beer that takes your fancy – herbs, spices, fruit... it's totally up to you. Buy pre-crushed malt if you don't want to grind it yourself (see below) and make sure there's plenty of room in your freezer for the hops.

Advanced option: Much as ground coffee beans quickly lose their oomph, barley will do the same – so buying a small malt mill will enable you to grind your own at the last minute and add more flavour, body and sugars to the brew right away. Similarly, you can pay through the nose for imported rare hops – so choose your recipes carefully!

OTHER ASSORTED THINGS

Add to your basic home-brew kit shopping list the following: **rubber** or **plastic bungs** (to seal up your conditioning vessel when you don't need the airlock), **plastic tubing** (to get wort from A to B), a **siphon** (to get your beer out of any buckets that lack fitted taps), a **large plastic spoon** (for stirring your mash), a **bottle filler** (a specific gadget to make filling bottles easier than with a tube) and plenty of **cleaning brushes**. For most of these, as they are reasonably cheap and you'll likely be relying on them a lot (and at critical "Where the f*** is it?" moments) you may want to buy multiples to be on the safe side.

EXTRACT BREWING
TAKING THE WHEEL (WITH STABILIZERS ATTACHED)

Before you lay down the cash for a malt mill and all kinds of other pro-style extravagancies, there is a type of brewing that can be performed on a budget and with relative ease – extract brewing. Instead of using grain and doing the mashing in yourself (see pages 126–7), you can buy a can of malt extract (a syrupy barley reduction, heavy with the sugars needed for fermentation) in which this stage of the process has been done for you. It's a short cut to home-brewing akin to tandem skydiving. You get the same rush, but under controlled circumstances. (OK, home-brewing may not be quite as exciting.)

Extract brewing skips the first step and proceeds directly to the boil – you simply tip the can into your stovetop pot (which takes a while, as you'll understand if you've ever poured treacle into anything), then heat it up, add the pelleted hops and cool the resultant wort before transferring and pitching the yeast. Kits that have extract in them usually come with a handful – literally sometimes – of real malt as well, for two very specific reasons:

A) these grains help boost the colour of your beer, if it's anything darker than golden; and

B) they give an idea of what brewing with real malt is all about.

There are many variations of extract-brewing kits available online or in your local home-brew retailer. Some have substituted the sticky can of syrup for a dried packet of pulverized grain (which has a longer shelf life); others have replaced the second step as well and are hopped malt extracts, so when you heat up the packet of powder with water you don't have to add hops.

These kits certainly streamline your brew-day and are much easier to get to grips with, but they also take the fun out of things along the way. Sure, they are cheaper and you get your beer fermenting away faster than if you go for all-grain – but whatever you end up with arrives through a much lesser degree of control. The personalization, experimentation and other freewheelin' aspects of home-brewing are deliberately kept to a minimum in the world of extract.

We're not against extract brewing per se – it's a start many of us have taken on the road to wherever our home-brewing adventures currently lie. But this freedom to tweak any and every part of the process is what makes brewing your own beer so awesome. It makes it harder, sure, and more prone to things going wrong – but the discoveries you make won't be as worthy if someone has taken care of the harder steps of the process for you.

As with tandem skydiving, there comes a time when you really need to take that leap on your own.

BREW IN A BAG

Having said that, there is another halfway house. Home-brewing is changing year on year – back in the day, the dividing line was between buying malt extract to heat up and serve or doing everything yourself (including your own welding and electrics). Now, though, there are other options for those just beginning their journey along the winding path to home-brew glory – and one of the more recent arrivals on the scene is the concept of "brew in a bag" beer making.

This is exactly what it sounds like: the great leap in DIY (do-it-yourself) brewing technology is a muslin sack. But what it means is that you need fewer pieces of kit, there are fewer steps in the process and you have a decent beer at the end of the operation. The major difference is that the mash and boil stages are undertaken in the same stovetop vessel, so you don't need a separate mash tun. This is to brewing what one-pot cooking is to the culinary world – it really is that simple.

All you need to do is heat the liquor in your pot to the correct temperature and drop the grains inside within the bag, so they sink into the hot water but can't escape. Once you've completed the mash you don't need to run off the wort – you simply pull the bag out instead. Then you've got a pot of wort sitting right in front of you, ready to be boiled. Heat up, add your hops, then cool and transfer for pitching the yeast. Easy!

Of course, there are negatives to this method – since you're not sparging on the fly, every drop of water used to mash in will be used for the boil (unlike pro brewers, who typically add more water at the start). So the efficiency of your brew-day will have to be monitored carefully and can vary greatly. Also the more obvious drawback is that you are limited in size based on what you can fit in the bag, whether the bag can fit in the pot and how heavy a load you can lift out (removing the wet bag is a hefty proposition).

But Brew in a Bag is actually a pretty faithful first step for those wanting to have a go at home-brewing – it's much more akin to the real thing than using extract, that's for sure. With less gear required it works out cheaper too; all you need is to be able to wash the bag afterward and you can go again. It allows you to experiment and add whatever you like to the mash, or boil, and as long as you don't let the bag stick to the inside of the pot and melt, it's pretty easy to clean up when you're done.

Most home-brew shops and online retailers sell everything you might need to make a start – including the all-important bags – but you can put them together yourself, if you have a material that's along the lines of a mosquito net. Although if you live in a country where mosquito nets are needed you might want to think twice before requisitioning yours to brew beer with. Priorities, and all that…

ALL GRAIN, NO PAIN

So, let's go.

You've got your kit, ingredients are prepped, your recipe is dialled in and you've loaded your MP3 player with smooth jazz. It's time to brew. Going all grain really is the best avenue to explore, and although it can seem daunting at first, there are plenty of resources online to help you through your brewday. Here's our guide to turning barley into beer without any fear.

MASH

First off, check what your grain looks like – if you have purchased pre-ground malt, you are good to begin brewing straight away. If your grains are whole, you'll need to mill them first. As we said before with the coffee analogy, buying whole grains (as with beans) gives you a richer flavour, but you have to crush them yourself before you can use them. Many home-brew shops (as with coffee roasters) will offer to mill your grain when you buy it – which is a good option if you plan to brew with it as soon as you get home.

Have all your gear ready to use (that is, cleaned and sanitized) and heat your water to 8°C (45°F) higher than whatever the mash temperature is on the recipe you are following. This is the strike temperature that gets things going, while balancing out the fact that everything is being done at room temperature. (You can get the same benefit by heating some water in the mash tun to warm the container, then throwing that water away.) Exactly how much water you'll need will depend on how much beer you are wanting to produce – but anything from 2–3 litres per kilogram of malt (about 68–100fl oz per pound) will be about right.

Once the mash water is at the right temperature, slowly pour in the crushed grains and get stirring. Keep on stirring for a good few minutes to let each and every kernel come into contact with your water and ensure there are no lumps. Slow and smooth is the order of the day. Your recipe will tell you for how long the grains are to steep in the mash – it will be at least an hour – and you should stir every 20 minutes while checking the temperature.

SPARGE

When the timer goes off, run off some of the mash and add it back to the top of the mash tun. This will help clarity by giving the particle-rich, sugary first runnings a chance to filter a bit more. You can keep running off until the wort is clear and lighter in colour. Then you are good to begin sparging. As a rough rule of thumb you'll need twice as much sparge water as mash water, so have it ready to go while the final minutes of the mash are ticking down. It should be as close to 76°C (170°F) as you can get it – this is very important as you'll remove the sugars but leave the bitter tannins behind in the grain husks.

Once you open the tap on the bottom of the mash tun for the wort to escape (down through a tube into your wort boiler), match the flow from this tap by adding sparge water on top of your warm grain bed. Never let it run dry at this point; always have a few centimetres (an inch or two) of liquid at the top of your mash tun. This way you won't simply be pouring sparge water straight through your grain; it will sit there and percolate, carrying those all-important sugars with it. The sparge will take between 45 minutes and an hour, and will result in a large pan of sweet wort ready to be boiled.

THE BOIL

Remove a small sample of your pre-boil wort and set it aside to cool. Once it has reached 20°C (68°F), check the gravity using your fancy new hydrometer. As it comes to a resting point you'll discover whether you have an efficient rate of extraction or not. If you've used the correct amount of malt and the ideal ratio of water, and have sparged correctly, you shouldn't be too far off (or you should be exactly on your target gravity). Carefully pick up your boiling vessel – it will have to have been below the level of your mash tun or you won't have got very far – and heat it on the stove to begin the boil.

At this point you can correct your gravity fluctuations by diluting with water (if the gravity was too high) or concentrating the sugars by boiling for longer (if too low). Measure out your hops while your wort is coming to a rolling boil. If you have produced more wort that you were expecting, you can always boil in two pots and do a split batch – this is a good opportunity to hop at different rates or even add other ingredients so that you end up with two beers for the price of one. Keep an eye on your pot and revel in the smooth, unhurried boil. If it looks as if it might boil over, turn the heat down a little.

Add your hops according to the timings on your recipe – you'll likely add the bittering hops very soon after the wort comes to the boil, and the aroma hops in stages later on. You may see particles floating around like a continually shaken snow globe – these are the long-chain proteins coming together due to the circular motion inside the pot (the coagulation is known as the hot break). It's OK – they eventually clump and gravitate towards the bottom of the pot – but keep an eye on it, particularly if it makes your wort bubble up a little more. Keep everything inside the pot!

HOPS

Your wort will also puff up again when the hops go in, so add them carefully rather than throwing in from a height. The bittering hops need at least an hour to release their tell-tale flavours, so put them in reasonably early at the stovetop stage. Add more as you go for the aroma, and any other ingredients if your beer has something else going on inside it. More likely than not these will be required toward the end of the boil – and it's a good idea to keep things like spices or fruit peels together inside a muslin bag (an old pair of tights also works – but be sure to ask the wearer's permission beforehand).

If you immediately transfer your freshly boiled wort into a fermentation vessel and pitch your yeast, you will end up with freshly boiled yeast – the single-celled organisms are miracle workers, but they aren't invulnerable and won't survive at the kind of temperature your wort is currently sitting at. So cool it down before transfer. You can do this in any one of a number of ways – the easiest is to walk away – but coil or plate chillers (see page 121) are much better, or there's the tried-and-tested method of placing your wort vessel in an ice bath. Once your pot is only just warm on the outside, it's yeasty time.

FERMENTATION

Transfer your wort into your sterile fermentation vessel and take a small sample aside to once again use with the hydrometer. Record your original gravity. Then it's time to pitch the yeast, so add rehydrated packet yeast at room temperature, or your trusty culture if you've managed to get one on the go, and carefully stir in with a sanitized spoon. From now on, anything that comes into contact with your wort (and then beer) must be sterile or you leave yourself open to all kinds of problems with infection. So resist the temptation to stir with your arm. It might be quicker than sterilizing a spoon, but is very bad.

Seal up your fermentation vessel with the lid and airlock and carefully transport the bucket somewhere to let the yeasts get on with their side of the business. Where you take it depends very much on what kind of beer you are brewing – obviously for a lager the yeast you have just added will need a cooler climate than a sugar-crazed ale yeast. The best place is a temperature-controlled fridge, so that you can monitor the ambient conditions exactly, but most beers will ferment quite happily at room temperature. It's sudden or obscene fluctuations that you want to avoid, as this will stress the yeast.

Chances are you'll be pressing your face to your fermentation vessel every few hours, like a kid at an aquarium tank, looking for the first telltale bubbles of CO_2 to appear. There's nothing wrong with this (unless you have steel vessels, that is), as keeping an eye on things will let you know when fermentation has finished and the bubbles frothing through the airlock have pretty much stopped. It could reach this point in anything from two days to a week. Once reached, you aren't done yet; although the vigorous stage has stopped, your beer – it is now beer – is ready to be conditioned.

SECONDARY FERMENTATION

Transfer your beer to another sterile vessel for this all-important conditioning phase. This takes a couple of weeks, to give the yeast time to re-absorb things like diacetyl and acetaldehyde, which make beer taste terrible, and to settle out and improve clarity. Any live yeasts will still be mixing it up in suspension, but their dead colleagues will have already sunk to the bottom of your primary fermentation vessel. So when you transfer the beer from first vessel to second, leave the sludgy mass of yeast and hops behind.

A LIFETIME OF BEER DISCOVERIES AWAITS, AND IT ALL BEGINS WITH THE POPPING OF THE CAP ON YOUR VERY FIRST HOME-BREW.

A rough rule of thumb is that the higher your recorded original gravity was, the longer you should leave your brew to condition – but if you leave it for a long time you might need to bottle-condition it to ensure that, when you get to drink it, the beer has a decent level of carbonation about it. Anyway, after a couple of weeks (so about three weeks in total, following pitching) the beer will have completed fermentation and be ready for priming – the addition of sugar. This ensures the carbonation levels in your home-brew will last for the duration of its bottled life and into your glass – the last thing you want is to have undergone all this time, effort and expense to end up with a flat, dull beer.

So unless you have some eye-wateringly expensive force-carbonation equipment (using gas), the addition of a specific amount of sugar to your batch is the way to go. Check online for calculations relating to your batch size – get this wrong and your beer may be enormously lively when the bottles are opened. You can prime into each bottle before filling or, if you have a bottling bucket, put your priming solution (a simple sugar and water solution) into it before adding the beer, and each bottle will have the same level of sugar added. All you need to do then is store the sealed bottles somewhere quiet and cool and wait a few days before sampling.

Congratulations! A lifetime of beer discoveries awaits, and it all begins with the popping of the cap on your very first home-brew. Now, where's that mash tun?

TROUBLESHOOTING

"Uh-oh. Something's not quite right with this one."

When the pit of your stomach is greeted not by tasty beer but by that sinking feeling instead, you know instantly that your home-brew is off the mark. Or maybe there's something happening (or not happening) during the brew-day that is causing you to scratch your head or shout profanities at the ceiling.

Home-brewing is hard – there are so many variables to consider, multiple processes to master, and you have the play of another creature to rely on for everything to turn out well. So when it doesn't, it can be a huge disappointment. But don't worry, every issue is a lesson to learn for next time. Here are a few of the more common brew-day dead ends, and how to avoid them…

STAGE: MASH

Problem: Stuck mash

HOW YOU KNOW

When you are mashing in and have plenty of liquid on top of your grain, but strangely nothing coming out of the tap at the bottom, you have a stuck mash (or more accurately, stuck sparge). Everything has ground to a gluey halt and you won't have much beer at the end of the brew-day.

WHAT TO DO

First, check the tap: it might be a simple blockage. If that doesn't help, sparge with hotter water (up to 80°C/175°F), as heat can help loosen the grain bed. If there's still no improvement, close your tap and stir the mash with more water (up to 80°C/175°F) if necessary, then begin run-off again. Be aware that following this the first runnings will be very cloudy and particulate-rich, so add them straight back to the top of the grain bed until the wort begins to run clear again.

STAGE: FERMENTATION

Problem: Blocked airlock

HOW YOU KNOW

Yeast is spraying out of the top of your fermenter.

WHAT TO DO

Fermentation can be a messy – and energetic – business, and sometimes the yeasts flurry away to such a degree that they want to take the party elsewhere, out of the airlock and into space. What happens, though, is that the delicate one-way valve of the airlock gets blocked. You'll have to remove it and use a blow-off valve instead (you can mock one up with a length of hose, run down and through a bucket of water on the floor). The yeast will bubble away and you won't have to steam-clean your ceiling.

Problem: Yeast dormancy

HOW YOU KNOW

Nothing is happening in your fermenter.

WHAT TO DO

Yeasts are extremely dependent on temperature (particularly those responsible for fruity ales) – if the ambient conditions become too cool for them to work effectively, they won't. So if your fermentation has stopped when it should still be going, move your fermenter to a warmer place and give the vessel a swirl to rouse the yeasts from their resting place at the bottom – this will hopefully spark them back into life and your airlock will soon be bubbling with the results.

STAGE: BEFORE TASTING

Problem: Your beer is overcarbonated

HOW YOU KNOW

The first bottle opened gushes foam everywhere.

WHAT TO DO

First get all of the beers into the fridge to cool down (this can obviously be done in batches if you have limited fridge space). Either you have added too much priming sugar and the yeasts are having a party, or you bottled the beer before they were done. Next time, cut down on the sugar and give the yeasts longer to work their magic. For this batch of beer you can uncap and then recap every one to let some of the pressure out, or just chill them and open over the sink when it's beer o'clock.

Problem: Your beer is cloudy

HOW YOU KNOW

Your beer is cloudy.

WHAT TO DO

This is something that can't be rescued, but for upcoming brewdays there are several ways to improve the clarity of your final beer. First, sparge for longer, with more recirculation of the wort to leave as much particulate from the grain behind as possible. Second, boil for longer and add Irish moss (a fining agent derived from seaweed) at the end of the boil. Third, cool the wort to a lower temperature after the boil, before you transfer it for fermentation. Fourth, add fining agents after fermentation to help clear the beer.

STAGE: TASTING

Problem: High levels of diacetyl

HOW YOU KNOW
Your beer tastes of popcorn, and is oily and slick.

WHAT TO DO
If your beer has already been bottled there's very little you can do, other than uncapping every one and adding more yeast to each. For next time, clean everything carefully (diacetyl can be a result of infection) and then, when you brew, lengthen your period of diacetyl rest – a few days should do it – to give the yeast sufficient time to think about what they have done and re-absorb the chemical.

Problem: High levels of dimethyl sulphide (DMS)

HOW YOU KNOW
Your beer smells like boiled corn (or maize) or tomato sauce.

WHAT TO DO
If you like your new vegetable-tinged beer, then nothing. If not, you need to have a more vigorous and prolonged boil next time around, to fully evaporate the DMS from your wort. You could brew with darker malt, as it has less DMS to begin with (the maltster having removed it in a similar manner during kilning), but most recipes contain plenty of pale malt, so work with your boil timings instead – and never boil in a closed container, or the volatiles will have nowhere to go.

Problem: High levels of acetaldehyde

HOW YOU KNOW
Your beer smells of sharp, green apples.

WHAT TO DO
This time around, there's nothing you can do – the yeast has been stressed and not been able to complete fermentation. Acetaldehyde is present in all beers to some degree – it is part of the pathway that leads from glucose to ethanol – but it needs to be kept to a minimum to stop your beer tasting like a citrus air-freshener. So for your next brewday, pitch an appropriate amount of yeast (i.e. more) and be patient with it – don't transfer your beer to the conditioning phase too quickly.

Problem: Bacterial infection

HOW YOU KNOW
Your beer has a vinegary tang, or eggy aroma.

WHAT TO DO
Throw it away – it is beyond help. Most home-brewers discover the need for thorough cleaning and sanitation the hard way, through this letdown when the first bottle of a batch is uncapped. Carefully sanitize each and every part of your equipment, and mentally revisit what you did post-boil that could have resulted in those pesky bacteria gaining a foothold and making their presence felt. Cleaning, cleaning, cleaning. That's the real work of a brewer.

Problem: Oxidation

HOW YOU KNOW
Your beer is dull, lifeless and smells and tastes of old books.

WHAT TO DO
Unless your home-brew has been in a cupboard for a few years, oxidation can wreak havoc on a beer if you aren't careful during the early stages of the brewing process. When lautering, take care to add the water carefully and not splash too much – ditto during the boil, which should roll but not splash. Otherwise, the aeration created by oxidation, combined with the elevated temperatures, acts on aldehydes in the wort that remain in the final beer and give it that unwanted papery, cardboardy flavour.

STAGE: FOLLOWING TASTING

Problem: You've been arrested

HOW YOU KNOW
Policemen are reading you your rights and telling you that home-brewing is illegal.

WHAT TO DO
If you are a budding home-brewer in Malaysia or Iran, then you might have to think again. In most countries where it *is* permitted, selling home-brew is a big no-no. Read up on your local laws while mashing in (you'll have time) and act accordingly. Send local lawyers a few samples, though, just in case.

ADVANCED MOVES
HOW TO TAKE YOUR HOME-BREW TO THE NEXT LEVEL

So, now that we can knock up a porter on a whim or a turbocharged IPA on a weekend, where next? Well, the beauty of home-brewing is that you are always learning – every brew-day teaches you something new. But if you are pretty confident in your own brewing ability, what can you do to push the boat out a little and challenge yourself?

Here are a few long-term projects to keep you busy – with the longest of all (growing your own hops) detailed in full on page 138. But while you are peering out of the window waiting for your personal stock of craft beer's most iconic ingredient, here are some other things to pass the time…

BUILD A KEGERATOR

We've talked about the switch to kegging from simple bottling, but if you decide to go for that if you're going to have to store the kegs somewhere cool while you drain them of their contents. And the best place for this is your own purpose-built custom kegerator. Find an old fridge (large enough to house your keg of choice and a CO_2 canister) and purchase a draft system – either one that can be mounted to the door or a tower system that can fit to the top. There are plenty of online guides to follow, and you'll end up with a homegrown minibar. You'll also suddenly be a lot more popular.

EMBRACE THE METAL

There's nothing that can't be achieved with cold, hard steel, and home-brewing is no exception. Ditch the plastic buckets and vessels and move away from glass carboys – go pro with stainless-steel vessels. Over time plastic becomes a haven for bacteria, anyway – the greater rigidity of metal will stand you in much better stead. Of course they come at a cost, but with a couple of small-scale conical steel vessels in your garage you can ferment and condition beer the way it was meant to be done.

HIT THE BOOKS

Brewing is 60% cleaning, 30% chemistry and 10% social media, and to really hit the heights of attenuation, yield and efficiency the middle one of those becomes enormously important. You can brew great beer with a working knowledge of chemistry, but if you take time and really study it the effect on your brews will be enormous. You'll be able to take full advantage of your water (or the water of other brewing regions) and monitor the pH of your creations at every step.

ALL DAY QA

In a similar vein, alongside training your brain to understand what's going on during the brew-day, you can also train your senses to fully appreciate and determine its effect on the results. The modern lab systems of craft breweries are way outside the home-brew spectrum, but our Quality Assurance programmes led by taste panels are not. Study flavour science, sit exams with bodies like the Cicerone® scheme, and become one with how beer should (and shouldn't) taste.

GET TOASTY

The process of kilning barley adds layers of flavour to the final beer, so those with a desire to experiment at home can re-create specific toasted malt characters using nothing more complicated than an oven and a baking tray. A centimetre (half-inch) depth of uncrushed pale ale malt heated for an hour at 150°C (300°F) will give toasty, roasted flavours – and if you soak the malt for half an hour first and "wet" roast it, it will verge towards the caramel. Don't forget to stir or shake the tray every five minutes when roasting, though.

GO SOUR

Culturing their own yeast is something that many home-brewers do as a matter of course – it gives greater consistency from batch to batch than dried yeast. But to move to the next level you could have a go at using funkier yeasts. You can buy them, but decanting from a bottle of Boon or Cantillon is more fun (for obvious reasons), and then you can pitch some of this after you've added your regular yeast. Sit back and wait, with the emphasis on waiting – if you bottle, be sure to open the first one with caution…

BARREL AGE

Oak chips or staves are great for introducing an "oak-aged" vibe to your homebrew (use about 30g per 20 litres/1oz to 5¼ gallons), particularly if you soak them in the desired spirit beforehand. But you can't beat the real thing. Getting hold of barrels can be tricky, but they don't just come in whisky-sized varieties; 20, 40 or 50-litre (5¼, 10½ or 13¼-gallon) versions do exist, and the fun of tracking them down becomes something dangerously close to an addiction. As does the desire to crack open the contents once your imperial barley wine has been inside for a year…

TOKYO*

INTERGALACTIC STOUT

A beer inspired by the ultimate arcade challenge – Space Invaders played in the mind-melting Japanese capital – Tokyo* is complex, and was surely released ahead of its time. The UK beer community at the end of the Noughties simply wasn't ready for a reverberating imperial stout a few points shy of 20% ABV. We were accused of irresponsibility, promoting alcoholism and causing the downfall of the Western World.

But what people didn't realize at the time is that strong beer is for savouring. Not shotgunning. It is all about moderation. Everything in moderation, including moderation itself. What logically follows is that you must, from time, have excess. Tokyo* is a beer for those times. It is for an armchair and tasting glass, for assessment. Careful thought and appreciation.

It is brewed with copious amounts of speciality malts, jasmine and cranberries. After fermentation it is dry-hopped with a bucketload of our favourite hops before being carefully aged on French toasted oak chips. The result is dark stone fruit, chocolate and coffee in abundance, together with vinous tartness from the berries.

Tokyo* has layer upon layer of complexity, and is a celebration of sensible, restrained drinking – it is the polar opposite of irresponsibility. More people than ever get that these days, which is a testament to how the perception of our beer industry has changed. If ever there were an antidote to overindulgence, then Tokyo* is it. A beer to relish, not to rush.

like that? try these:

PÉCHÉ MORTEL

9.5%

Dieu du Ciel!, Canada

Intensely dark and roasty stout, a "mortal sin" to be savoured

SAINT PETERSBURG

7.4%

Thornbridge, England

Pitch black and perfectly balanced from start to (long) finish

SPEEDWAY STOUT

12%

AleSmith, USA

World-class imperial stout lifted by the addition of coffee

RELISH, DON'T RUSH

RELEASED	2008
ABV	16.5%
STYLE	IMPERIAL STOUT
IBU	85
HOPS	CHINOOK, GALENA, FIRST GOLD
MALT	EXTRA PALE, DARK CRYSTAL, CHOCOLATE, ROASTED BARLEY

"MY FAVOURITE THING ABOUT TOKYO* HAS ALWAYS BEEN THE NEWSPAPER HEADLINE IN THE TIMES THAT HAD A PICTURE OF JAMES NEXT TO A HEADLINE SAYING 'BINGE DRINKING: BLAME THIS MAN'." — MARTIN DICKIE

"MY INTRODUCTION TO AMPLIFICATION. NEVER BEFORE HAD A BEER BOTH ENLIGHTENED AND CONFUSED ME SIMULTANEOUSLY. SILENCED BY ITS BRILLIANCE, TOKYO* IS SIMPLY A LITTLE BIT SPECIAL." — EQUITY PUNK OLIVER BOULTON

DROPTICK
TICK THIS BEER OFF YOUR LIST WITH A DROP FROM YOUR FINGER

YOU SAY:

....
....
....
....
....
....

GROW YOUR OWN

There's no two ways around it – the cost of buying hops can add up over time. So if your credit card shrinks in fear at the prospect of another trip to the home-brew store, maybe your back garden can provide the solution. Cut out the middleman and grow your own. If you have a space that gets plenty of sun and where the climbing plants can get a vertical workout, then it's actually not as crazy as it sounds.

Hops are restricted to certain latitudes because of their need for daylight, but those parts include large swathes of northern and central Europe, North America, Asia and Australasia. The right varieties will even grow in Scotland, given the right conditions.

The two things all hops need are between six and eight hours of sunlight each day, and well-drained soil that has plenty of nutrients to feed their climbing habit. If you can't guarantee that amount of rays where you are, they will still grow – you'll just end up with fewer cones to harvest.

But for home-brewers, it's not about a commercial-grade supply, so anything that can be sourced from the garden can be used to make up the numbers in a brew that would otherwise have to be paid for! Plus you'll find that the hops best suited to your part of the world can be used to re-create your local styles.

So if you live in the North of England (for example), you can use a harvest of uniquely English hops such as Target or First Gold to produce a quintessential bitter or golden ale, giving a new outlook on your hobby if you normally rely on imported Chinook or Citra.

Hops grow from rhizomes, small roots that burrow through the soil and can end up supporting a plant 6m (20ft) high (albeit with a bit of help from something to hang on to). Planted in the spring with a climbing trellis to conquer, they can do what they do best.

They need plenty of water, and you can help your yield by selecting the best-looking bines and wrapping them around their climbing structure to give them an advantage. Cut the rest of the shoots away and the plant will give all its attention to the ones racing skyward!

Harvest your crop – such as it is – in late summer by picking the cones that are dry and covered in the golden dust that gives them their flavour. Dry them further in a warm spot inside, out of the sunlight to help stop that flavour being leached away before you have a chance to unlock it.

If you don't get many (or any at all), don't despair. As long as the plant has grown and looks healthy, chances are you will get a better harvest in year two. Once all the cones are gone, cut the bine to about 1m (3ft) high and then cut again to ground level in winter.

The beauty of hops is that if you look after them and can give them a microclimate of sun and lots of water, they will allow you to produce all manner of different beers. If the idea of your own garden-grown fresh-hop beer appeals, it might not be an impossible dream…

HUMULUS LUPULUS
ASPECT: HOT, SUNNY, OPEN

CASCADE
Aroma Hop
- GRAPEFRUIT
- FLORAL
- SPICY

WILLIAMETTE
Aroma Hop
- FRUITY
- HERBAL
- CITRUS

NUGGET
Aroma/Bittering Hop
- HERBAL
- SPICY
- STONE FRUIT

ASPECT: COOL, SUNNY, BREEZY

FIRST GOLD
Aroma/Bittering Hop
- FLORAL
- ORANGEY
- STONE FRUIT

CHALLENGER
Aroma/Bittering Hop
- SPICY
- WOODSY
- EARTHY

TARGET
Aroma/Bittering Hop
- CITRUS
- SPICY
- FLORAL

HOW TO HOST A BEER TASTING

GLASSES? CHECK. BOTTLE OPENER? CHECK.

On the face of it, hosting a beer tasting is a simple matter – as long as you have more than one beer, more than one person and pour yourself slightly larger measures than anybody else, you are pretty much good to go. But to run an event that gets all your friends enthused about the myriad different options present in the world of beer and opens eyes as well as bottle caps, there are a few things that you can do.

So find your sturdiest kitchen table (or compile one from the wooden pallets your beer order arrived on) and dig out the wipe-clean tablecloth. If you follow the six following principles then you won't go too far wrong – unless the extravagantly packaged Belgian quad takes out your 65in UHD TV with an unfortunate "point and shoot" cork accident. Remember most household insurers won't pay out for over-carbonation…

GO VERTICAL

What initially seems like common sense – going from weakest to strongest in your beer lineup over the course of the evening – actually has many different pathways. Aside from ensuring that people haven't knocked back the Double IPAs before they've taken their shoes off, moving up through the alcohol levels gives your guests' palates time to attune to the beer load over the course of the evening.

But that's a simple way of looking at it – these days there are plenty of session-strength beers that pack a walloping flavour, whether through the bitterness levels, addition of chillies or whatever. So when the time comes to arrange the tasting bottles, take everything into account and come up with an order of play that gives every beer a chance to shine and doesn't allow one to dominate the entire evening.

PERFECT SERVE

You need to have the beer at the ideal condition when it's go time. There's no other reason people came round, after all. So check the preferred temperature for the styles you have and take the bottles or cans out of the fridge with plenty of time to spare. This lets their flavours shed the cloak of anonymity that beers tend to pick up in the refrigerator (if in doubt, serve at a cool 10–12°C/50–54°F).

Small tasting glasses are the way to go. In order not to overload everyone, use "three from 330ml (12fl oz)" as a rule of thumb in terms of pouring amounts. And this is generous – if you are hosting a barley wine evening, dial it back a bit more. Also be mindful of bottle-conditioned beers when dishing out the samples. You should leave the sediment behind when pouring and taste the beer without but it is interesting to also taste the beer with the characteristic flavour of the sediment to gain a greater understanding of how the added yeast can fundamentally change a beer.

GET REFRESHED

A beer tasting should be an enjoyable marathon, not a sprint marred by people running outside of their lanes. So make sure all attendees have unlimited access to water with which to rehydrate, cleanse their palates and clean their glassware in between rounds. Unless you have a truly colossal beer glass collection, rinsing from beer to beer is the best way to avoid flavour cross-contamination.

Have on hand things for your guests to chew on – as a bare minimum, plain crackers to act as reset. But other snacks will be welcomed, and some high-quality cheese is a great boost to bring out when people are flagging and the imperial stouts have appeared. Plus it acts as another indication of how one set of flavours influences another.

MAKE A NOTE

At this point, the discussion during and after the beer tasting can go in many different directions (in proportion to the number of beers sampled). But there's little point in just knocking the beers back in silence, so why not take the opportunity to chat about how the flavours and aromas are coming through from each one, and whether your guests enjoyed one more than another?

People love to quantify things, so give them a pencil and a scoring sheet (like the one opposite) and let them have at it. This is not simply to justify your awesomeness at choosing beers; it will give them a chance to work out what styles they like if they aren't so sure, and also record for their own posterity any beers they fall in love with over the course of the evening.

LOOK FOR MISTAKES

Even with the best will in the world, brewers sometimes get things wrong (or things go wrong when the beer has left their hands). Off-flavours often raise their ugly, unwanted heads when you're tasting several beers of similar type in quick succession, so for added beer-tasting-evening points make a few notes on some of the more frequently encountered, just in case you get that telltale whiff of popcorn, green apples or vinegar.

And for even more points, you can purchase kits of pre-mixed capsules containing said off-flavours online (they are what we use to train our taste panels and would-be tasters on the Cicerone® scheme). Hosting a special off-flavour tasting evening is an utterly fascinating way to build an olfactory library of faults that will help in your future tastings (especially if you are a home-brewer).

HOST A BLIND TASTING

This is really the ultimate, and a tasting that will brilliantly summarize what you and your buddies have deciphered from the numerous beer tastings you have taken part in previously. What you see obviously has a big bearing on what you taste and enjoy, so with that removed from the equation, your other senses will have to step up (and take it from us – they really do).

So find a willing volunteer to pour and distribute the beers unseen in unmarked glasses, and have at it. You could even blindfold yourselves so the colour of the beer doesn't come into play. What can you smell? Can you pick the individual hops? Is there a style that you lean toward for each beer? Why not write down what type of beer you think it might be (removing the blindfold first, if you value your tablecloth)?

RATE YOUR BEER

BEER NAME:

BREWERY:

ABV _____ STYLE _____ COUNTRY _____

TASTING DATE _____ TASTED BY _____ BOTTLE OR CAN? _____

WHO BROUGHT IT? _____ HOW MUCH? _____ WORTH IT? _____

APPEARANCE
_____
_____
_____
_____
_____

AROMA
_____
_____
_____
_____
_____

FLAVOUR
_____
_____
_____
_____
_____
_____

MOUTHFEEL
_____
_____
_____
_____
_____
_____

AFTERTASTE
_____
_____
_____
_____

OTHER NOTES
_____
_____
_____
_____

WOULD GO GREAT WITH
_____
_____

TRIED & TASTED!
AND I SCORED IT
/10

DIY DOG
GIVING IT ALL AWAY

The spirit of home-brewing is ingrained deeply into our DNA at BrewDog. The original brewery in Fraserburgh was basically just a giant home-brewing setup, with plastic water tanks and completely manual controls. We learned how to work it from the ground up, using trial and error, by putting in the hours in all weathers. Very much like a home-brew!

Many of the classic BrewDog beers were developed during those early days, and we still use a 50-litre (13¼-gallon) home-brew system to develop new beers and new recipes. Anyone can make amazing beer, on even the smallest set-up – particularly with the shared knowledge, expertise and passion that flows through the craft brewing and home-brewing communities. It is a sense of collaboration that we have always wanted to take to the next level.

So in early 2016, we did, with DIY Dog.

With DIY Dog we wanted to do something that had never been done before, as well as paying tribute to our home-brewing roots. We took all of our recipes and gave them away for free to the amazing global home-brewing community. After all, we had turned home-brewing into a career – so hopefully others following in our path could use our recipes to do the same.

For generations, companies have fiercely protected their "secret" recipes – clinging to the classified, yellowing documents nervously hidden away by the founders, keys to the safe around their necks. The plodding remnants of another age desperately hang on to their foundations while businesses born in the 21st century realize it is all about sharing. Build your community by being open and inclusive, not protective. Who cares about 11 herbs and spices? Really, these days?

We released the detailed instructions to 234 of our beers: the keys to our kingdom – every single BrewDog recipe, ever. For the express purpose of allowing home-brewers to copy them, tear them to pieces, bastardize them, adapt them – but most of all, enjoy them. DIY Dog is anti-corporate beer writ large, a new way of doing business. Released as a free download, it was our way of giving back to the community that helped us out with advice, support and feedback before BrewDog was even a thing.

So we want to continue that spirit by including the recipes to ten of our beers within these pages. Never before published in hard-copy format together, they can be enjoyed by anyone with a homebrew kit. We have also reached out to our friends in the craft brewing community, and they have given us recipes to their beers for you to try at home as well.

Spread the word; share the love. Enjoy.

PUNK IPA

POSTMODERN CLASSIC

ABV 5.6%   **IBU 35**   **OG 1053**

BREWDOG   ELLON, UK

Punk IPA. Amplified. In 2010 we finally got our paws on the equipment we needed to dry-hop our beers. We then focused all our energy on dry-hopping, amping up the aroma and flavour of our flagship beer to create a relentless explosion of tropical fruits, and adding a hint of Caramalt to balance out the insane amount of hops.

BASICS

VOLUME	20L	5.3gal
BOIL VOLUME	25L	6.6gal
ABV		5.6%
TARGET FG		1011
TARGET OG		1053
EBC		15
SRM		7.6
PH		4.4
ATTENUATION LEVEL		78%

METHOD/TIMINGS

MASH TEMP
66°C   152°F   75 mins

BOIL TIME
60 mins

FERMENTATION
19°C   66°F   variable
(see page 130)

BREWER'S TIP

To get the best possible profile from the dry hops we recommend dry-hopping post fermentation for five days. For maximum aroma, add dry hops at cellar temperature, around 14°C (57°F).

FOOD PAIRING

Spicy carne asada with
    a pico de gallo sauce
Cheesecake with
    a passion-fruit swirl sauce
Chicken wings
    (see recipe on page 183)

INGREDIENTS

 MALT

Extra Pale	4.38kg	9.6lb
Caramalt	0.25kg	0.55lb

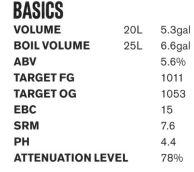 **HOPS**

Variety	(g/oz)	Add	Attribute
Chinook	20/0.71	Start	Bitter
Ahtanium	12.5/0.44	Start	Bitter
Chinook	20/0.71	Middle	Flavour
Ahtanum	12.5/0.44	Middle	Flavour
Chinook	27.5/0.97	End	Flavour
Ahtanum	12.5/0.44	End	Flavour
Simcoe	12.5/0.44	End	Flavour
Nelson Sauvin	12.5/0.44	End	Flavour
Chinook	47.5/1.7	Dry Hop	Aroma
Ahtanum	37.5/1.3	Dry Hop	Aroma
Simcoe	37.5/1.3	Dry Hop	Aroma
Nelson Sauvin	20/0.71	Dry Hop	Aroma
Cascade	37.5/1.3	Dry Hop	Aroma
Amarillo	10/0.35	Dry Hop	Aroma

 YEAST

Wyeast 1056 – American Ale™

5AM SAINT

BITTERSWEET CHAOS

ABV 5%　　**IBU 35**　　**OG 1050**

BREWDOG　　ELLON, UK

Five AM is The Holy Grail of red ales. We live in a world of disposable deities. Someone, somehow has managed to press that big, flashing moronic override button and we are hardwired straight into the pockets of false idols trying to make a quick buck. Once this ruby liquid forms a foamy halo around your glass, you will never want to look back.

BASICS

VOLUME	20L	5.3gal
BOIL VOLUME	25L	6.6gal
ABV		5%
TARGET FG		1012
TARGET OG		1050
EBC		60
SRM		30.5
PH		4.4
ATTENUATION LEVEL		76%

METHOD/TIMINGS

MASH TEMP
62°C　144°F　75 mins

BOIL TIME
60 mins

FERMENTATION
19°C　66°F　variable
(see page 130)

BREWER'S TIP

Go easy on the crystal and dark crystal malts. Too much will skew the flavour profile away from lychees and citrus towards dried fruit.

FOOD PAIRING

Cheddar cheese melt on crisp rye toast
Moroccan chicken tagine
Cheesecake topped with kiwi fruit

INGREDIENTS

 MALT

Extra Pale	2.56kg	5.6lb
Caramalt	0.88kg	1.9lb
Munich	0.63kg	1.4lb
Crystal 150	0.38kg	0.83lb
Dark Crystal	0.13kg	0.28lb

 HOPS

Variety	(g/oz)	Add	Attribute
Cascade	2.5/0.09	Start	Bitter
Amarillo	2.5/0.09	Start	Bitter
Nelson Sauvin	2.5/0.09	Middle	Flavour
Amarillo	12.5/0.44	End	Flavour
Nelson Sauvin	12.5/0.44	End	Flavour
Simcoe	25/0.88	Dry Hop	Aroma
Cascade	50/1.8	Dry Hop	Aroma
Ahtanum	25/0.88	Dry Hop	Aroma
Nelson Sauvin	12.5/0.44	Dry Hop	Aroma
Centennial	50/1.8	Dry Hop	Aroma
Amarillo	25/0.88	Dry Hop	Aroma

 YEAST

Wyeast 1056 – American Ale 11™

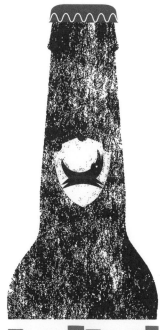

DEAD PONY CLUB

WEST COAST KICKS

ABV 3.8% **IBU 40** **OG 1040**

BREWDOG   ELLON, UK

Our California-style West Coast IPA has light toffee and caramel notes layered on biscuit malt. These support a huge fresh citrus aroma, with lemongrass, lime zest and grapefruit peel, alongside some tropical notes, courtesy of heavy-hitting US hops.

BASICS

VOLUME	20L	5.3gal
BOIL VOLUME	25L	6.6gal
ABV		3.8%
TARGET FG		1012
TARGET OG		1040
EBC		25
SRM		12.7
PH		4.4
ATTENUATION LEVEL		70%

METHOD/TIMINGS

MASH TEMP
62°C   144°F   75 mins

BOIL TIME
60 mins

FERMENTATION
19°C   66°F   variable
(see page 130)

BREWER'S TIP

It may be tempting to throw extra (extra) hops at Dead Pony Club, but try adding a little at a time to consecutive brews rather than cramming in loads on your first attempt.

FOOD PAIRING

Baja-style fish tacos
Jerk chicken
Apple crumble

INGREDIENTS

MALT

Extra Pale	2.79kg	6.14lb
Caramalt	0.63kg	1.38lb
Crystal 150	0.19kg	0.41lb

HOPS

Variety	(g/oz)	Add	Attribute
Simcoe	5/0.18	Start	Bitter
Citra	5/0.18	Start	Bitter
Simcoe	5/0.18	Middle	Flavour
Citra	5/0.18	Middle	Flavour
Simcoe	50/1.8	Dry Hop	Aroma
Citra	75/2.6	Dry Hop	Aroma
Mosaic	62.5/2.2	Dry Hop	Aroma

YEAST

Wyeast 1056 – American Ale™

KINGPIN

21ST CENTURY LAGER

ABV 4.7%   **IBU 40**   **OG 1044**

BREWDOG   **ELLON, UK**

A 4.7% German Pils with light, biscuit and toasty malt character, upon which is built a hop bitterness that provides complexity and a long, dry finish. The fact that lager now tastes of nothing is a 500-year-old fallacy. Our cold-conditioned king is proof that lager can taste of something, and then some.

BASICS

VOLUME	20L	5.3gal
BOIL VOLUME	25L	6.6gal
ABV		4.7%
TARGET FG		1008
TARGET OG		1044
EBC		14
SRM		7
PH		4.2
ATTENUATION LEVEL		79%

METHOD/TIMINGS

MASH TEMP
65°C   149°F   75 mins

BOIL TIME
60 mins

FERMENTATION
10°C   50°F   variable
(see page 130)

BREWER'S TIP

Keep an eye on your fermentation temperature to ensure you get the crisp notes that are the hallmark of a good Pilsner.

FOOD PAIRING

Jamaican jerk chicken wings
Corn dogs
Strawberry ice-cream sundae

INGREDIENTS

 MALT

Pilsner	1.63kg	3.58lb
Caramalt	0.16kg	0.36lb
Munich	0.63kg	1.38lb
Pale Malt	1.50kg	3.30lb

 HOPS

Variety	(g/oz)	Add	Attribute
Magnum	5/0.18	Start	Bitter
Perle	25/0.88	Middle	Flavour
Perla	12.5/0.44	End	Flavour

 YEAST

Wyeast 2007 – Pilsen Lager™

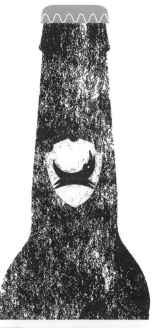

JACK HAMMER

RUTHLESS IPA

ABV 7.2%   **IBU 250**   **OG 1065**

BREWDOG   ELLON, UK

Hopped beyond the point at which IBUs are measurable, only the most hardened palate wil get beyond Jack Hammer's intensely resinous pithy bitterness to the grapefruit, orange zest and dry, biscuity malt beneath. You could brew this with fewer hops, but really, why would you bother?

BASICS

VOLUME	20L	5.3gal
BOIL VOLUME	25L	6.6gal
ABV		7.2%
TARGET FG		1010
TARGET OG		1065
EBC		15
SRM		7.5
PH		4.4
ATTENUATION LEVEL		84.6%

METHOD/TIMINGS

 MASH TEMP
65°C   149°F   75 mins

 BOIL TIME
60 mins

 FERMENTATION
21°C   70°F   variable
(see page 130)

BREWER'S TIP

Be aware that this is probably the hoppiest beer you will ever make. Make sure you use fresh hops for a massive fresh grapefruit hit. Have everything else to hand and buy the hops last, as close to brew-day as possible.

FOOD PAIRING

Phall curry
Pork burrito with a habanero and mango chilli salsa
Ginger and grapefruit pound-cake

INGREDIENTS

 MALT

Extra Pale	5.81kg	12.8lb

 HOPS

Variety	(g/oz)	Add	Attribute
Centennial	25/0.88	Start	Bitter
Columbus Extract	30/1.1	Start	Bitter
Centennial	18.75/0.66	Middle	Flavour
Columbus	18.75/0.66	Middle	Flavour
Centennial	50/1.8	End	Flavour
Columbus	25/0.88	End	Flavour
Amarillo	100/3.5	Dry Hop	Aroma
Citra	100/3.5	Dry Hop	Aroma
Simcoe	100/3.5	Dry Hop	Flavour

 YEAST

Wyeast 1272 – American Ale 11™

ELVIS JUICE

CITRUS INFUSED IPA

ABV 6.5% **IBU 60** **OG 1060**

BREWDOG   ELLON, UK

Punchy, resinous, hoppy aromas blast from your glass; light floral and citrus notes riff against huge piney character, showcasing Citra, Simcoe and Amarillo at their absolute best. A huge dose of grapefruit peel brings swirls of fresh pithy zest, accentuating the dry hops and building on the dry, biscuity malt base.

BASICS

VOLUME	20L	5.3gal
BOIL VOLUME	25L	6.6gal
ABV		6.5%
TARGET FG		1010
TARGET OG		1060
EBC		25
SRM		12.5
PH		4.4
ATTENUATION LEVEL		83.3%

METHOD/TIMINGS

MASH TEMP
65°C   149°F   75 mins

BOIL TIME
60 mins

FERMENTATION
19°C   66°F   variable
(see page 130)

BREWER'S TIP

Shave off the surface of a citrus peel to unlock the highly aromatic compounds into the beer. Avoid adding any white pith, though, as it will create an intense and unpleasant bitterness.

FOOD PAIRING

Mexican ceviche
Coriander and lime green Thai curry
Grapefruit soufflé.

INGREDIENTS

 MALT

Extra Pale	4.5kg	9.9lb
Caramalt	0.88kg	1.92lb

 HOPS

Variety	(g/oz)	Add	Attribute
Magnum	2.5/0.09	Start	Bitter
Simcoe	12.5/0.44	Middle	Flavour
Amarillo	12.5/0.44	Middle	Flavour
Mosaic	25/0.88	End	Flavour
Citra	25/0.88	End	Flavour
Amarillo	12.5/0.44	End	Flavour
Simcoe	12.5/0.44	End	Flavour
Citra	50/1.8	Dry Hop	Aroma
Amarillo	50/1.8	Dry Hop	Aroma
Simcoe	50/1.8	Dry Hop	Aroma

YEAST
Wyeast 1056 – American Ale™

TWIST

Add as much grapefruit and orange peel as you dare to the FV for extra citrus impact.

ELECTRIC INDIA

VIBRANT HOPPY SAISON

ABV 5.2%   **IBU 38**   **OG 1045**

BREWDOG   ELLON, UK

One of our most popular seasonal beers, Electric India appeared originally as an Equity Punk shareholder creation and retains its trademark spicy, fruity edge. A perfect blend of Belgian saison and US IPA, crushed coriander seeds and heather honey are also added to give a genuinely unique beer.

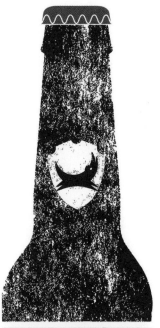

BASICS

VOLUME	20L	5.3gal
BOIL VOLUME	25L	6.6gal
ABV		5.2%
TARGET FG		1005
TARGET OG		1045
EBC		15
SRM		7.5
PH		4.4
ATTENUATION LEVEL		88.9%

METHOD/TIMINGS

MASH TEMP
65°C   149°F   75 mins

BOIL TIME
60 mins

FERMENTATION
22°C   72°F   variable
(see page 130)

BREWER'S TIP

Source some really good heather honey to get the right spicy esters for this beer.

FOOD PAIRING

Mussels with a garlic and herb sauce
Crab melt sandwich
Shortbread cookies

INGREDIENTS

 MALT

Extra Pale	3.63kg	7.98lb
Munich	0.13kg	0.28lb
Wheat	0.25kg	0.55lb

HOPS

Variety	(g/oz)	Add	Attribute
Amarillo	2.5/0.09	Start	Bitter
Nelson	5/0.18	Middle	Flavour
Amarillo	5/0.18	Middle	Flavour
Peppercorns	2.5/0.09	Middle	Flavour
Nelson	20/0.71	End	Flavour
Amarillo	12.5/0.44	End	Flavour

 YEAST

Wyeast 3711 – French Saison™

TWIST

	(g/oz)	Add
Honey	62.5/2.2	End, Whirlpool
Coriander Seeds	8.5/0.3	45mins

HELLO MY NAME IS INGRID

SOPHISTICATED BERGMANESQUE BEER

BREWDOG   ELLON, UK

One thing is certain: this Swedish-inspired Double IPA is not as innocent as she first appears. A seductive body of rich malts and a buxom amount of Columbus, Centennial, Nelson Sauvin and Bramling Cross hops have been added to fresh Scandinavian cloudberries to deliver this beer's tart finish.

ABV 8.2%   IBU 42   OG 1078

BASICS

VOLUME	20L	5.3gal
BOIL VOLUME	25L	6.6gal
ABV		8.2%
TARGET FG		1013
TARGET OG		1078
EBC		70
SRM		35
PH		4.4
ATTENUATION LEVEL		83.3%

METHOD/TIMINGS

MASH TEMP
65°C   149°F   75 mins

BOIL TIME
60 mins

FERMENTATION
22°C   70°F   variable
(see page 130)

BREWER'S TIP

Grind the cloudberries to a paste to extract maximum flavour and add them when you are racking the beer after primary fermentation.

FOOD PAIRING

Crayfish with a chilli and coriander-
    infused butter dip
Smørrebrød or other dark bread with
    cream topping
Cardamom cake with powder sugar and
    cloudberry jam

INGREDIENTS

 MALT

Maris Otter Extra Pale	6.86kg	15.10lb
Caramalt	0.93kg	2.05lb

 HOPS

Variety	(g/oz)	Add	Attribute
Columbus	25/0.88	Start	Bitter
Centennial	25/0.88	Start	Bitter
Columbus	12.5/0.44	End	Flavour
Centennial	12.5/0.44	End	Flavour
Nelson Sauvin	25/0.88	End	Flavour
Bramling Cross / First Gold	37.5/1.3	End	Flavour
NZ Nelson Sauvin	71.5/2.5	Dry Hop	Aroma
Bramling X	71.5/2.5	Dry Hop	Aroma
Simcoe	71.5/2.5	Dry Hop	Flavour

YEAST

Wyeast 1272 – American Ale 11™

TWIST

Cloudberries	1kg/ 2lb 4oz

AB:04

IMPERIAL STOUT WITH COFFEE, LOADS OF COCOA & CHILLI

ABV 15% **IBU 80** **OG 1113**

BREWDOG   ELLON, UK

Imperial Stout brewed with coffee, cocoa, Naga chillies (the hottest in the world) and champagne yeast. Possibly our most acclaimed Abstrakt of all time.

BASICS

VOLUME	20L	5.3gal
BOIL VOLUME	25L	6.6gal
ABV		15%
TARGET FG		1018
TARGET OG		1113
EBC		400
SRM		200
PH		4
ATTENUATION LEVEL		84.1%

METHOD/TIMINGS

 MASH TEMP
63°C   154°F   90 mins

 BOIL TIME
60 mins

 FERMENTATION
21°C   70°F   variable
(see page 130)

BREWER'S TIP

Make sure you can get the coffee, cocoa and chillies out of the beer when the flavours are right.

FOOD PAIRING

Beef machaca on corn tortillas
Chilli and dark chocolate tart
Epoisses cheese

INGREDIENTS

 MALT

Pale Ale Malt	10kg	22.03lb
Wheat Malt	0.94kg	2.06lb
Flaked oat Malt	1.88kg	4.13lb
Dark Crystal 350	1.25kg	2.75lb
Chocolate	0.94kg	2.06lb
Black Patent	0.94kg	2.06lb

 HOPS

Variety	(g/oz)	Add	Attribute
First Gold	75/2.6	Start	Bitter
Fuggles	75/2.6	Start	Bitter
Fuggles	62.5/2.2	End	Flavour
Coffee Beans	37.5/1.3	End	Flavour

 YEAST

Wyeast 1272 – American Ale 11™

TWIST

Add a muslin bag containing 50g (1¾oz) coffee beans, 25g (1oz) raw cacao beans and as many Naga Viper chillies as you dare to the cold conditioning and remove at the end.

PARADOX ISLAY

UBIQUITOUS IMPERIAL STOUT

ABV 10%   **IBU 100**   **OG 1090**

BREWDOG   ELLON, UK

In 2006 James and Martin persuaded acclaimed beer writer Michael Jackson to taste one of their home-brews – the first incarnation of the now-ubiquitous Paradox. Aged in a variety of casks over the years, Paradox is dark, decadent and encapsulating. Can be enjoyed fresh; phenomenal when aged.

BASICS

VOLUME	20L	5.3gal
BOIL VOLUME	25L	6.6gal
ABV		10%
TARGET FG		1014
TARGET OG		1090
EBC		300
SRM		152
PH		4.4
ATTENUATION LEVEL		84.4%

METHOD/TIMINGS

MASH TEMP
65°C   149°F   90 mins

BOIL TIME
60 mins

FERMENTATION
21°C   70°F   variable
(see page 130)

BREWER'S TIP

The beauty of this beer lies in how brilliantly it lends itself to infusing or ageing. Experiment with different additions while the beer is ageing, taste it regularly to gauge its progress, and make sure you package it at its peak.

FOOD PAIRING

Ancho chilli beef taco
Chocolate gateau
Rum-poached pears with
    dark chocolate sauce

INGREDIENTS

 MALT

Extra Pale	4.5kg	10lb
Caramalt	0.55kg	1.2lb
Munich	0.33kg	0.7lb
Flaked Oats	1.35kg	3lb
Dark Crystal	0.55kg	1.2lb
Carafa Special Malt Type 1	0.18kg	0.4lb
Carafa Special Malt Type 3	0.33kg	0.7lb

 HOPS

Variety	(g/oz)	Add	Attribute
Columbus	75/2.6	Start	Bitter
Columbus	25/0.88	Middle	Flavour
Saaz	25/0.88	End	Flavour
First Gold	25/0.88	End	Flavour

 YEAST
Wyeast 1272 – American Ale 11™

TWIST

Try ageing on oak chips and infusing with vanilla pods or rum-soaked raisins.

One of the unspoken wonders of craft beer is the sense of community that exists within the industry. Companies that are essentially in competition with each other have a level of respect seldom seen elsewhere. We had wanted to extend this DIY Dog chapter to include home-brew recipes of ten guest beers, each produced by an amazing brewery we know and admire greatly. But we weren't sure that any of them would be willing to part with their crown jewels, the bedrock of what makes them who they are.

We needn't have worried. Every single one said yes immediately.

As with BrewDog, the history of many (if not all) of these companies is deeply rooted in home-brewing. As a result, the recipes of their beers – some of which on the following pages have never been published before – are not sacred. When the aim is to give back to the next generation of home-brewers experimenting in their kitchens or garages, this incredible spirit comes out. So here, for your home-brewing pleasure, are some truly astounding beers to re-create – from one beer community to another.

GAMMA RAY

ABV 5.4% **IBU 45** **OG 1051**

AMERICAN PALE ALE
BEAVERTOWN   LONDON, UK

Gamma Ray is big, hoppy and fresh: a perfect example of a hop-forward pale ale. Juicy American hops added in ever-increasing amounts at the end of the boil and in the fermenter give huge flavour and aroma to this modern classic.

BASICS

VOLUME	20L	5.3gal
BOIL VOLUME	25L	6.6gal
ABV		5.4%
TARGET FG		1010
TARGET OG		1051
EBC		16
SRM		8
PH		4.4
ATTENUATION LEVEL		80%

METHOD/TIMINGS

MASH TEMP
66°C   152°F   70 mins

BOIL TIME
60 mins

FERMENTATION
19–21°C   66–70°F
variable (see page 130)

FOOD PAIRING

Vietnamese spring rolls

INGREDIENTS

 MALT

Extra Pale	4kg	9lb
Caramalt	0.21kg	0.46lb
Caragold	0.12kg	0.25lb

HOPS

Variety	(g/oz)	Add	Attribute
Columbus	7/0.25	Start	Bitter
Columbus	8/0.28	End (WP)	Flavour
Mosaic	8/0.28	End (WP)	Flavour
Bravo	8/0.28	End (WP)	Flavour
Amarillo	8/0.28	End (WP)	Flavour
Citra	52/1.8	Dry Hop, 20°C	Aroma
Amarillo	42/1.5	Dry Hop, 20°C	Aroma
Calypso	16/0.56	Dry Hop, 20°C	Aroma

 YEAST

Fermentis US–05

DARK ARTS

SURREAL STOUT

ABV 6% **IBU 30** **OG 1060**

MAGIC ROCK HUDDERSFIELD, UK

Dark Arts blends four malts and bags of whole hops to deliver a decadently deep and indulgent experience. A luxuriously smooth mouthfeel is followed by spicy hop notes and full flavours of chocolate, liquorice, blackberries and figs. The finish is rich and satisfying with a lingering roasted bitterness.

BASICS

VOLUME	20L	5.3gal
BOIL VOLUME	22L	5.8gal
ABV		6%
TARGET FG		1014
TARGET OG		1060
EBC		59
SRM		30
PH	4.7, start of fermentation	
ATTENUATION LEVEL		77%

METHOD/TIMINGS

 MASH TEMP
68°C   154°F   60–75 mins

 BOIL TIME
90 mins

 FERMENTATION
17–20°C   62–68°F
variable (see page 130) increase to the higher temperature towards the end of fermentation

FOOD PAIRING

Barbecued meat – try slow-cooked ribs

INGREDIENTS

 MALT

Golden Promise	3.8kg	8.4lb
Brown Malt	0.175kg	0.39lb
Black Malt	0.175kg	0.39lb
Chocolate Malt	0.175kg	0.39lb
Oats	0.175kg	0.39lb

 HOPS

Variety	(g/oz)	Add	Attribute
Magnum	7/0.25	Start	Bitter
Target	35/1.2	Dry Hop, for 7 days	Aroma
Hurkules	35/1.2	Dry Hop, for 7 days	Aroma

YEAST

WLP001 – California Ale

FORTUNATE ISLANDS

AMERICAN WHEAT ALE

MODERN TIMES　　**SAN DIEGO, USA**

ABV 5%　　**IBU 46**　　**OG 1046**

Fortunate Islands shares the characteristics of an uber-hoppy IPA and an easy-drinking wheat beer. A massive dose of Citra and Amarillo hops gives it a blast-wave of tropical hop aromatics: mango, tangerine and passion fruit all leap out of the glass.

BASICS

VOLUME	20L	5.3gal
BOIL VOLUME	35L	9.2gal
ABV		5%
TARGET FG		1007
TARGET OG		1046
EBC		7.7
SRM		3.9
PH		4.5
ATTENUATION LEVEL		82%

METHOD/TIMINGS

MASH TEMP
65°C　149°F　20 mins

BOIL TIME
60 mins

FERMENTATION
20°C　68°F
variable (see page 130)

FOOD PAIRING

Spicy street tacos

INGREDIENTS

MALT

Pale Malt	1.8kg	4lb
Wheat Malt	1.64kg	3.62lb
CaraVienne Malt	0.14kg	0.31lb
Acid Malt	0.07kg	0.16lb

HOPS

Variety	(g)	Add	Attribute
Citra	4.75/0.17	Start	Bitter
Citra	18.2/0.64	Middle	Flavour
Amarillo	9/0.32	Middle	Flavour
Citra	98/3.5	Dry Hop, 7 days	Aroma
Amarillo	25/0.88	Dry Hop, 7 days	Aroma

YEAST

Wyeast American Ale #1056

HOP DEVIL

INDIA PALE ALE

ABV 6.7% **IBU 65** **OG 1065**

VICTORY BREWING COMPANY
DOWNINGTON, PENNSYLVANIA, USA

Hop Devil is one of the original East Coast IPAs, probably the first to use German Vienna malts and whole-flower American hops. It is piney, resinous and rich with malt character. At over 60 IBUs, it is a serious balance of malts and hops.

BASICS

VOLUME	20L	5.3gal
BOIL VOLUME	23L	6.1gal
ABV		6.7%
TARGET FG		1016
TARGET OG		1065
EBC		33
SRM		17
PH		4.25
ATTENUATION LEVEL		75%

METHOD/TIMINGS

MASH TEMP
65°C	149°F	(10min rest)
72°C	162°F	(40min rest)

BOIL TIME
60 mins

FERMENTATION
18–20°C   64–68°F
variable (see page 130) then add
10 days cold storage at 0–2°C
(32–36°F)

FOOD PAIRING
Philly cheesesteak

INGREDIENTS

 MALT

Vienna Malt	3.29kg	7.25lb
Crystal 150	0.17kg	0.375lb

 HOPS

Variety	(g/oz)	Add	Attribute
Cascade	6/0.21	Middle	Flavour
Centennial	3/0.11	Middle	Flavour
Cascade	10/0.35	End	Aroma
Fuggles	10/0.35	End	Aroma
Centennial	5/0.18	End	Aroma
Cascade	60/2.1	Hop Back	Aroma
Fuggles	60/2.1	Hop Back	Aroma
Centennial	60/2.1	Hop Back	Aroma

YEAST
Wyeast American Ale #1056

AKA IPA

INDIA PALE ALE

ABV 6.7%   **IBU 60**   **OG1063**

CROMARTY BREWING COMPANY   CROMARTY, UK

Released without fanfare in November of 2012, this India Pale Ale from Cromarty Brewing Company remains one of the best IPAs in the UK, with a nigh-perfect tipping point from citrus into sticky resin. The fascinating baseline of malt from around the globe allows the brewer to then (in Cromarty's words) "lash hops at it".

BASICS

VOLUME	20L	5.3gal
BOIL VOLUME	23L	6.1gal
ABV		6.7%
TARGET FG		1012
TARGET OG		1063
EBC		17
SRM		9
PH		4.5
ATTENUATION LEVEL		80%

METHOD/TIMINGS

 MASH TEMP
64°C   147°F   60-90 mins

BOIL TIME
90 mins

 FERMENTATION
20°C   68°F
variable (see page 130)

FOOD PAIRING

Fatty cheese such as a mature Brie

INGREDIENTS

MALT

Maris Otter	4.35kg	9.59lb
Crystal	0.28kg	0.62lb
Munich Malt	0.20kg	0.48lb
Wheat	0.12kg	0.26lb

HOPS

Variety	(g/oz)	Add	Attribute
Perle	5/0.18	Start	Bitter
Dana	5/0.18	Middle	Flavour
Columbus	5/0.18	Middle	Flavour
Cascade	25/0.88	End	Aroma
Columbus	25/0.88	End	Aroma
Perle	25/0.88	End	Aroma
Dana	25/0.88	End	Aroma
Cascade	38/1.3	Dry Hop	Aroma
Columbus	25/0.88	Dry Hop	Aroma
Dana	12/0.42	Dry Hop	Aroma

YEAST

WLP001 – California Ale

BERGAMOT HOPFEN WEISSE NO. 1

GERMAN-STYLE WHEAT IPA

ABV 6.5% **IBU 28** **OG 1060**

CLOUDWATER   MANCHESTER, UK

Floral, pungent and hoppy, this beer combines two classic global styles – the German Weissbier and the US IPA. Never afraid to experiment, Cloudwater then added the juice and zest of bergamot lemons – and such was the public reaction that this version (first introduced as part of their debut spring 2015 range of beers) was re-brewed and released again, to the same level of acclaim.

BASICS

VOLUME	20L	5.3gal
BOIL VOLUME	25L	6.6gal
ABV		6.5%
TARGET FG		1010
TARGET OG		1060
EBC		22.7
SRM		11.5
PH		4.01
ATTENUATION LEVEL		81%

METHOD/TIMINGS

MASH TEMP
67°C   153°F   60 mins

BOIL TIME
90 mins

FERMENTATION
19.5°C   67°F
variable (see page 130)

FOOD PAIRING

Lightly steamed white fish such as cod or haddock

INGREDIENTS

 MALT

Best Ale Malt	2.1kg	4.6lb
Wheat	3.9kg	8.6lb
Light Munich	0.1kg	0.24lb
Caramalt	0.1kg	0.24lb

 HOPS

Variety	(g/oz)	Add	Attribute
Perle	17/0.6	Start	Bitter
Citra	150/5.5	End, WP	Flavour
Citra	100/3.5	Dry Hop, for 7 days	Aroma

 YEAST

Fermentis WB06

TWIST

	(g/oz)	Add	Attribute
Bergamot Lemon, chopped	70/2.5	End, WP	Flavour
Kaffir Lime Leaf, 1 or 2 leaves		End, WP	Flavour
Bergamot Lemon, chopped in muslin sack	300/10.5	Dry Hop, when beer has fermented to 1018	Aroma

HALCYON

IMPERIAL IPA

ABV 7.4%   **IBU 70**   **OG 1070**

THORNBRIDGE BREWERY   BAKEWELL, UK

For nearly ten years Halcyon has been flying the flag for UK-brewed imperial IPA, and it shows no sign of slowing down. The balance of different hops into a crescendo of tropical, berry and citrus flavours is unique and leaves a beer that is incredibly easy to drink at over 7% ABV!

BASICS

VOLUME	20L	5.3gal
BOIL VOLUME	25L	6.6gal
ABV		7.4%
TARGET FG		1013
TARGET OG		1070
EBC		12
SRM		6
PH		4.3
ATTENUATION LEVEL		80%

METHOD/TIMINGS

 MASH TEMP
68°C   154°F   60 mins

 BOIL TIME
75 mins

 FERMENTATION
20°C   68°F
variable (see page 130)

FOOD PAIRING

Strong French cheese

INGREDIENTS

 MALT

Pale Ale Malt	6.5kg	14.3lb

 HOPS

Variety	(g/oz)	Add	Attribute
Warrior	50/1.8	Start	Bitter
Bramling Cross	60/2.1	End	Aroma
Nelson Sauvin	40/1.4	End	Aroma
Galaxy	20/0.71	End	Aroma
Chinook	20/0.71	End	Aroma
Ella	20/0.71	End	Aroma
Nelson Sauvin	70/2.5	Dry Hop	Aroma
Cascade	50/1.8	Dry Hop	Aroma
Galaxy	40/1.4	Dry Hop	Aroma
Ella	40/1.4	Dry Hop	Aroma

YEAST

WLP001 – California Ale

SMOKED PORTER

SMOKED PORTER

ABV 5.9%   **IBU 53**   **OG 1065**

STONE BREWING   SAN DIEGO, USA

Although Stone are masters of the hop, their darker releases are also way ahead of the curve. First released in the weeks leading up to Christmas of 1996, Stone Smoked Porter is dark, smooth and complex, with chocolate and coffee flavours suffused with subtle smokiness from the addition of peat-smoked malt.

BASICS

VOLUME	20L	5.3gal
BOIL VOLUME	23L	6.1gal
ABV		5.9%
TARGET FG		1018
TARGET OG		1065
EBC		69
SRM		35
PH		4.5
ATTENUATION LEVEL		58%

METHOD/TIMINGS

MASH TEMP
69°C   156°F for 10 min, then raise to 74°C 165°F

BOIL TIME
90 mins

FERMENTATION
22°C   72°F
variable (see page 130)

FOOD PAIRING

Stuffed mushrooms

INGREDIENTS

 MALT

Pale Malt	4.56kg	10.06lb
Crystal Malt	0.53kg	1.17lb
Chocolate Malt	0.30kg	0.66lb
Peat-Smoked Malt	0.14kg	0.31lb

 HOPS

Variety	(g/oz)	Add	Attribute
Columbus	20/0.71	Start	Bitter
Mt Hood	17/0.6	End, WP	Flavour

 YEAST

White Labs WLP007 Dry English Ale or WLP002

IMPERIAL BLACK

IMPERIAL BLACK IPA

ABV 7.5% **IBU 82** **OG 1072**

BUXTON BREWERY   BUXTON, UK

Black IPA burst onto the scene a few years ago, offering the best of two very different worlds – the hop-forward citrus and resin of the IPA and the smooth roastiness of dark ales. Buxton's Imperial Black is one of the originals and one of the very best, balancing every flavour to perfection.

BASICS

VOLUME	20L	5.3gal
BOIL VOLUME	23L	6.1gal
ABV		7.5%
TARGET FG		1015
TARGET OG		1072
EBC		60
SRM		30
PH		4.4
ATTENUATION LEVEL		79%

METHOD/TIMINGS

 MASH TEMP
65°C   149°F   90 mins

 BOIL TIME
75 mins

FERMENTATION
18–21°C   64–70°F
variable (see page 130) raise to the higher temperature after 48 hours

FOOD PAIRING

Freshly shucked oysters

INGREDIENTS

 MALT

Pale Ale Malt	3.9kg	8.6lb
Munich Malt	0.34kg	0.75lb
Dark crystal	0.25kg	0.55lb
Carafa III spread over the completed mash prior to sparging	0.20kg	0.44lb

 HOPS

Variety	(g/oz)	Add	Attribute
CO_2 hop extract (Columbus)	11/0.39 at 47.94% Alpha	Start	Bitter
Citra	50/1.8	End	Aroma
Simcoe	25/0.88	End	Aroma
Citra	60/2.1	Dry Hop	Aroma
Simcoe	60/2.1	Dry Hop	Aroma

 **YEAST**
West Coast Pale Ale

IT'S ALIVE

BELGIAN WILD ALE

ABV 8%   **IBU 60**   **OG1065**

MIKKELLER   COPENHAGEN, DENMARK

Mikkeller's answer and tribute to the Queen of Trappist beers – the iconic Orval – is easy to drink and has a serious amount of hops in the recipe. Once brewed, this beer demands to be served in the Belgian way – poured with high, white dense foam in your best glassware. As is it part-fermented with Brettanomyces, be sure to clean your home-brew kit extra carefully once you're finished!

BASICS

VOLUME	20L	5.3gal
BOIL VOLUME	25L	6.6gal
ABV		8%
TARGET FG		1004
TARGET OG		1065
EBC		20
SRM		10
PH		4.3
ATTENUATION LEVEL		93%

METHOD/TIMINGS

 MASH TEMP
64°C   147°F   60 mins

 BOIL TIME
60 mins

 FERMENTATION
23-24°C   73-75°F   variable
(see page 130)

FOOD PAIRING

Prosciutto di Parma

INGREDIENTS

 MALT

Pale Malt	3.65kg	8.05lb
Caramalt	0.59kg	1.30lb

 HOPS

Variety	(g/oz)	Add	Attribute
Zeus	15/0.53	Start	Bitter
Saaz	20/0.71	Middle	Flavour
Saaz	25/0.88	End, WP	Flavour
First Gold	60/2.1	Dry Hop	Aroma

 YEAST

WLP510 Bastogne Belgian Ale; Yeast Brettanomyces brux ellensis

TWIST

	(g/oz)	Add	Attribute
Candy Sugar (light)	750/26	End, WP	Body

#MASHTAG

DEMOCRATIC BEER MAKING

Brewing is far from a solitary pursuit. Even those who ply their trade as individuals or who home-brew on their own are backed by a legion of others: the farmers who grow the barley, wheat and hops; the maltsters who then convert the raw grain into fuel cells for a brewer's yeast; the engineers who construct the brew kit – and, of course, last but very definitely first – the beer fans who enjoy the outcome.

The vast majority of breweries are staffed by dedicated people whose skills and experience intermesh into the ultimate team. For them, making beer is done as a group, a collective, and the bottles, kegs or casks that leave the brewhouse at the end of the process are far better as a consequence. We love the fact that our crew is tight-knit, committed and fanatical.

And the same goes for our beer fans – which is why we let them take the reins too.

#MashTag is crowd-sourced brewing writ large. Since 2014 we have turned over every aspect of one beer a year to our customers – each single element of the brew is their call. They have final say on all decisions. From the individual style at the beginning right up to the label art for the bottles – it's all down to our fans. We put the options to them, and they choose the path the beer will take.

Here's a snapshot of how it works, from the 2015 competition…

DAY ONE THE BEER STYLES	DAY TWO MALT BILL & ABV	DAY THREE HOPS & IBU	DAY FOUR THE TWIST
Pale Ale	**10% Black Barley Wine**	European Hops 65 IBU	Belgian Yeast
Stout	12% Barley Wine	**US Hops 100 IBU**	**Oak Chips and Vanilla**
Barley Wine	7% 'Session' Barley Wine	UK Hops 35 IBU	Cascara and Dark Berries

We love handing the keys of our Ellon brewery over to the people who eventually end up drinking the beer (not that our brewers don't enjoy the odd beverage every now and again). It's like giving a car club a thousand pencils and asking them to design the next convertible. Sure, there are going to be some fairly out-there ideas coming back, but you're going to get something amazing.

Variety is very much the crux of the matter – and our #MashTaggers never seem to disappoint with their choices. After all, when given a trolley and the chance to dash around a supermarket, you don't load up with 40 packets of cornflakes. Our annual design-a-beer-by-committee spectacular is a chance for beer drinkers to pin back their collective ears and go for it.

Over the years, #MashTag has resulted in beers as diverse as a brown ale aged on oak chips and hazelnuts, a sour cherry triple IPA and an imperial black vanilla barley wine. The week-long frenzy of collective recipe-making is a tradition accepted with flair and style, and that's long before we ask for budding artists to submit their ideas for label art…

#MASHTAG 15

A 10% US-HOPPED BLACK BARLEY WINE WITH ADDED VANILLA BEANS AND TOASTED OAK CHIPS AND ARTWORK DESIGNED BY MARK GREEN

DOG
EAT DOG

BEER & FOOD:
THE HOW & THE WHY

Craft beer may be the reason we get up in the morning, but one can't live on beer alone. Thankfully, great food goes really well with great beer – a fact now being discovered by increasingly more people. Wine may claim the high ground, but the era of it being an integral part of dinnertime is over.

Pairing beer and food is a call to arms gaining traction with each passing month – rejecting the idea that the only option at mealtime is to reach unthinkingly for the corkscrew. We would respectfully argue on behalf of something else with subtlety, flavour and class to act as a foil for whatever is on your plate.

It's time for beer to sit at the top table.

One of the main reasons why is its versatility, due to the sheer number and variety of styles. Terroir, varietals and vintage all play a part when it comes to grapes – but also to hops. On top of this beer can then have a multitude of malt bills, a raft of possible extra ingredients, the action of barrel-ageing, differing yeasts or even souring bacteria.

The irony is that we have always known beer and food go well together – you have only to cast your mind to television and images of medieval feasts, modern-day summer barbecues or the "pie and a pint". All feature beer at their core; it's as if its inclusion at mealtimes has been whitewashed – or winewashed – from public consciousness.

And yet the second irony related to this is the one mantra we all remember about wine and food pairing: "red with meat, white with fish". How dumbed down is this, for the complex, upmarket grape? Beer and food go together better than anything else you can eat and drink at the same time, because it has such a weight of variety behind it.

Truth is, beer's variety can sometimes be problematic. With so many variables in play there are far more factors to take into account when selecting a beer to go with your food; the different hops, malt grains, strains of yeast, added ingredients, serving methods and alcohol-by-volume levels, to name but a few. So where to begin? Well – the best place is in beer's equivalent of the "red or white?" question…

What kind of beer do I want to drink tonight?

Above all else this is the most vital choice. The decision of what style of beer is going home with you will enable you to shape that perfect pairing (assuming you are starting with the beer, as opposed to making a shop run with a half-made meal simmering away on your stove top).

From bready German Pilsners to tub-thumping Double IPAs, Belgian fruit beers to deeply roasty imperial stouts – all have cuisine(s) that will bring out the very best in the beer, and in turn, the food.

But to achieve pairing nirvana, there are three simple concepts to follow: beery laws designed to balance your food and drink as carefully as that pile of dishes in the sink…

1. INTENSITY

The first of these notions is easy to get your head around. It may be obvious, but when scanning the shelves of the beer aisle, select something that is of the same intensity as the meal you are planning at home.

So if you're going to enjoy a subtle, refined dish with delicate or muted flavours, best leave those barrel-aged imperial porters on the shelf – they will dominate and blow the food out of the metaphorical water. The beer will be all you will taste. Likewise, there's no point bringing a crisp floral lager to a Stilton party.

So far, so common sense. The potential issue is that the list of multiple variables we talked about earlier comes into play. The concept of "intensity" doesn't just equate to "alcohol strength" – if you have a strongly flavoured meal in the pan, picking a beer with double-digit ABV could well work, but there's no guarantee.

And that's because with beer, matching "intensity" means you need to take account of everything else as well: how roasty that imperial porter is from the malt bill, whether any other ingredients have been let loose, how bitter the hop load is, whether it's been barrel-aged and so on. Oh, and the second issue is that unfortunately there's no such thing as a Stilton party. Although there definitely should be.

This latent complexity also applies to the food that you are going to eat, of course – particularly if you are approaching this chicken-and-egg pairing from the point of view of the meal rather than its liquid accompaniment. A lightly poached piece of fish is going to demand a more delicate beer pairing than a dry-rubbed, 20-hour slow-roasted rack of ribs.

You can match those two dishes nicely as they stand – poached fish goes really well with Pilsner and a slab of ribs is the ideal companion for a Scotch ale. But just as you should think about the extras in the beer for an advanced food pairing, so too you need to consider whatever else is going on in the dish. For instance, if that fish is laden with a sauce it will add an entirely new dimension to the equation.

From zingy salad dressings to nuclear-level, sign-a-waiver vindaloo, the addition of gravies, foams and anything else chef can dream up is intended to change the flavour of the dish, otherwise they wouldn't be on the plate – so your choice of beer will have to change accordingly. And that is where the second perfect pairing rule comes into play…

2. FLAVOUR

Following on from intensity, we have the next priority. If a meal and a beer possess a similar flavour (or even share an exact ingredient), then chances are they will pair off very nicely indeed.

So let's take another look at that Scotch ale you picked up from the shelf. Ignore the faux tartan on the label and instead read the blurb on the back of the bottle. Hmm. It's been barrel-aged, so has an added layer of oaky, vanilla flavours on board. And it's also had coffee beans included in the recipe. So a sweet boozy coffee beer. What could we pair with that?

Well, how about the classic Italian dessert tiramisu? The beer would go brilliantly as it shares all of the flavour peaks – the sweetness on the finish from that barrel-ageing will result in a similar flavour to the Marsala wine in tiramisu, and it's a no-brainer that the coffee in both would square off with each other in the very best of ways.

And yet, matching flavours to great effect needn't be this precise. If you are preparing a meal containing cherries, then a Belgian kriek would fit the bill nicely. These historic beers have cherries added into the barrels while they are maturing, with the juice and tartness from the fruit leaching into the beer as a result. Hungry beer drinkers can then take advantage of the brewer's craft.

Matching two similar flavours in a dual-pronged pairing is kind of like that Pairs game you used to play with animal cards, back in the day. Remember where that zebra card was, so that when its partner appears you can head straight back and pick up both of them. Flavour matching is a memory game – and not one that you need necessarily play while standing in the aisles of a supermarket, either.

Flavour association is something you can practise irrespective of whether you are having a bite to eat. Each time you try a new beer and think "Ooh, that tastes of…" remember what that thing was (peaches, chocolate, coriander leaves) and store the information in the memory banks for the next time you plan a stone-fruit dessert, rich torte or fragrant Asian soup.

As with the intensity rule, once the principles of flavour matching have become clear, it can be taken up a level. So, even if the food and beer have no identifiable ingredients in common at all, the techniques employed by brewer and/or chef can result in complementary flavour profiles to aid the pairing. Let's look back (longingly) at that rack of dry-rubbed, 20-hour ribs.

What are the main flavours you would expect from that slab of low and slow beef? Meaty, obviously. Roasty. Sweet, from the barbecue sauce. Smoky from the oven. So if you are after a beer to go alongside, look for something featuring caramel malt flavours, like a German Doppelbock. Or majoring on the smoke – a Rauchbier. Or aim for the dry and roasty angle, with a Schwarzbier. And yes, with roasted meat it's not a coincidence that all of these beers are German.

3. CONTRAST

Finally, the third thing to bear in mind when selecting a beer to go with your dinner (or lunch, or breakfast) is to work with – or against – the contrasting components of both.

So this moves beyond matching broad intensities and instead looks for high-level characteristics like richness, fattiness or spicy heat. These can then either be balanced to great effect, or offset to lift or calm as required and still result in a satisfying beer and food experience.

Let's look at an example: spicy heat. Heat is balanced by sweetness and malt in a beer but is actually emphasized by hop bitterness. So that nuclear vindaloo will be kept in check by a rich, malty Belgian Trappist dubbel but will run roughshod over your palate when paired with a bitter, hoppy IPA.

Yes – IPA makes curry hotter. If that sounds surprising (and painful), then select a beer that has a higher malt level and lower hop bitterness to compensate for the heat. If you are dead set on that hop bomb to go alongside your curry, break out a stronger, sweeter US double IPA instead – or better still, a barley wine. These malt-led beers are perfect foils for spicy heat.

Barley wine and curry is an example of using high-level contrast to cut through a potentially dominant part of a meal – but others exist too. Whereas hops draw attention to heat, they also act to reduce sweetness – as in the classic (if seldom tried) beer and food pairing of India pale ale and carrot cake. No, really. The hop bitterness of the IPA cuts through the sweetness of the icing.

This kind of contrast may leave you the subject of strange glances in tearooms ("I don't think they are drinking Darjeeling, Gladys"), but they really do work. Just think of the one overwhelming facet of the food in question – so, with carrot cake, the sweetness – and pick something that is as far removed from that in beer terms as you can get. The opposite sensation from sweetness: bitterness.

So to return to the cherry-based dish discussed earlier, Belgian kriek would be a fantastic complementary pairing, but for a contrasting angle take the dominant component and flip it in the other direction. With sharp, fruity cherries, counterpoint with a roasty, chocolaty imperial stout instead. Does that leave you thinking of Black Forest cake? Absolutely, and that's why that dessert works so well.

With beer and food pairing, the bottom line is that if you can match the intensity, flavours and contrasts then you won't go far wrong. And when starting out, whatever beer you select – as long as it's one you enjoy – will help you learn and come to future tables with great pairings.

After all, the process requires nothing more than eating amazing food and drinking world-class beer. Well, plus the odd bit of dishwashing…

EAT WITH BEER

Speaking of dishwashing, here are 20 reasons to reach for the rubber gloves. The first ten are easy-to-cook dishes to be paired with amazing beer; the second ten go a step further, each using beer as an ingredient in the cooking process (minus a small amount for taste purposes, obviously . . .)

PAD THAI & SAISON DUPONT

Spice?... Think Fragrant
Beer Style: Saison

Thai food delivers hit after hit after hit to the taste buds, dishing out a pounding from the vibrancy of chilli, coriander leaves, lemongrass and fish sauce. Asian food in general is a good match for highly hopped beers, but the complex elements of Thai cuisine are best paired with a beer that can deliver more. A beer like a saison. The classic Belgian saison Dupont works really well with a pad thai; the peppery spice and soft yeast esters match the savoury nam pla and sweet palm sugar at each and every turn.

Open a bottle of Saison Dupont from the fridge and pour it into a clean glass. Take in the aroma of citrus and light stone fruit, pepper and esters from the yeast. The flavours will follow suit, growing more complex as the beer warms to room temperature while you are dancing with your sturdiest wok. Pad thai is a dish to be made quickly, smashing the ingredients around over a high heat and then wolfing it down while the temperature still stings the throat. When that moment arrives, your glass of now cellar-cool saison will be your reward – and the perfect accompaniment.

Put the tamarind paste into a hot wok with the palm sugar and fish sauce. Once the sugar has dissolved, taste it. You can add chilli now or later, depending on how hot you like things, but once you're happy with the sauce, pour it into a bowl. Clean the wok with kitchen paper, add a dash of oil and crank up the heat.

You'll also want to prepare the noodles at this point, so either pause for a minute or get someone to add them to boiling water and then drain them. Add a little of your freshly made sauce and stir, to stop them drying out and sticking together.

Now brace yourself at the cooking station and start tipping things into the hot oil. Start with the prawns. If they are raw they'll obviously need longer than if pre-cooked (if frozen, put them into a small plastic bag in a bowl of boiling water when you're at the sauce stage). Add the tofu as well – when the prawns are cooked, and the tofu browned, remove everything from the wok and tip into a bowl.

Dash more oil into the pan and cook the shallot, chilli (if not added earlier) and sliced garlic. Once the aromas are flooding your kitchen, it's really go time. Stir in the noodles and sauce, then add the cooked prawns and tofu. Get everything moving and crack an egg over the lot – scrambling it up and mixing it into the noodles.

The final addition is everything you have left – the bean sprouts, garlic chives and peanuts. Once thoroughly mixed and cooked through, decant to bowls and serve with the lime wedges and saison.

SERVES 2

Ingredients:

1 tablespoon tamarind paste
1 tablespoon palm sugar
4 teaspoons nam pla (fish sauce)
1 red chilli, finely sliced, seeds in or out – your call
vegetable oil
100g (3½oz) flat rice noodles
8 large peeled prawns, or lots of smaller ones
75g (2½oz) tofu, cut into cubes
1 shallot, sliced
1 large garlic clove, sliced
1 egg
50g (1¾oz) bean sprouts
4 stalks of garlic chives, chopped
50g (1¾oz) unsalted peanuts, chopped
lime wedges, to serve

OTHER BEERS TO TRY

Fantôme Saison,
Ommegang Hennepin,
BrewDog Electric India

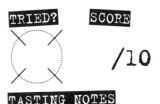

TRIED?   SCORE

/10

TASTING NOTES

CITRUS & PARMESAN RISOTTO & SCHNEIDER WEISSE ORIGINAL

Richness?... Think Wheat
Beer Style: Hefeweizen

Richness can mean many things, but for this recipe we are talking about all things buttery, glossy and creamy. Great to eat, but tough to pair a beer with – you need a sturdy hop monster to stand up to a rich dish, or the beer will be overpowered. However, there is an alternative – you can go in the other direction and match like with like by pouring a German-style Hefeweizen. The creaminess in your bowl is equalled by the smoothness of the wheat, and with both having a kick of citrus they are perfect together.

Back in the day, the German beer purity law that stipulated a standard of ingredients had but a single loophole – it also allowed the use of wheat for Weizens brewed by the Bavarian royal family. Eventually these rights were claimed by a single commercial brewery – Georg Schneider & Sohn (the son was also named Georg). They saved, protected and popularized this style, and now German Hefeweizen has taken over the world – yet Schneider Weisse is the original. Open a bottle and enjoy the banana, clove, spice and citrus aromas and flavours – the latter of which is the key to this pairing.

Soften the shallots and garlic in a pan with plenty of butter (or a 50/50 mix of butter and oil) and when translucent, add the dry rice. Ensure all the grains are coated, and after they in turn start to become translucent – a process you can stand there and watch, if you like – add a healthy splash of the wine and the stock and stir. Put on the lid, and you have begun the addition/reduction face-off that creates the perfect risotto. Check every so often (no longer than 5 minutes), moving things around, and when dry add more of both liquids, stir and replace the lid.

About halfway through your supply of stock and wine, leave both where they are and add the lemon juice instead. Then go back to the other liquids and add a mixture of both, as before, until the rice is cooked and ever-so-slightly chewy (or you can let it go past the al dente stage and fully cook – it's your call). When the grains are just how you like them, mix in the lemon zest, Parmesan and parsley and season to taste with salt and pepper.

Serve with the beer, which is now produced by the great-great-great grandson of the founder (and his name, as you may have guessed, is also Georg Schneider).

SERVES 2

Ingredients:

2 shallots, diced
1 garlic clove, diced
a couple of knobs of butter
200g (7oz) arborio rice
500ml (18fl oz) white wine
500ml (18fl oz) vegetable stock
juice and grated zest of 1 lemon
20g (1oz) grated Parmesan cheese
a small handful of fresh parsley, chopped
salt and pepper

OTHER BEERS TO TRY

Weihenstephaner Hefeweissbier,
Ayinger Bräu-Weisse,
Sierra Nevada Kellerweis

TRIED?   SCORE

/10

TASTING NOTES

STEAMED COD WITH DILL & BREWDOG KINGPIN

`Herbs?... Think Floral`
`Beer Style: Pilsner`

The continued slight against lagers is that they don't taste of much – so given that, how can you pair them with food? Well, as we have seen, well-made lager styles actually feature a range of flavours – grassy, floral and even slightly herbal. So if you are thinking of dining on something that can enter the same bracket, it's time to uncap a Pilsner or helles. Subtly herbed white fish is an all-time lager classic; imagine you're on the sun-blasted deck of a seaside restaurant and you'll enjoy it even more.

Kingpin is our take on the quintessential German Pils, so once taken from the fridge and allowed to warm to a cellar-cool temperature, open the bottle (or can) and pour into the tallest, thinnest glass you have in your collection. The aromas of bready, biscuity malt are joined by a citrus and floral element which really comes through on the taste – particularly the grapefruit and lemon bitterness. This alone makes it a perfect foil (pun intended; see later) for white fish, and the herbal hit from the dill and parsley in this recipe will emphasize the corresponding flavours in the beer even more.

This recipe couldn't be easier. Preheat the oven to 180°C/355°F/gas mark 4. Now take a large square of foil and place the chunky cod fillet in the centre (any white fish that flakes will do, really). Season it on both sides with salt and pepper and add a quarter of the dill, parsley and spring onion on top. Top with a slice of lemon and a knob of butter, and crimp the foil parcel into a shape that will allow the steam from the fish to rise up and be retained in the parcel. If you want to be extra beery you can add a generous splash of Kingpin before sealing instead of the butter – this will really get the flavours running through the fish. Repeat to make 3 more parcels with the other fillets.

Bake the fish until it is cooked through and just starts to flake apart when you open the foil and poke it with a fork. Depending on the size of your fillets (which will shrink during cooking), this could be between 10 and 20 minutes, so once your kitchen timer hits double digits, check the fish every couple of minutes until it is cooked all the way through – i.e. opaque and without any translucent parts in the centre.

Serve with some green vegetables and the Kingpin alongside; close your eyes in between bites and you can almost hear the seagulls wheeling overhead.

SERVES 4

Ingredients:

4 large sustainable cod fillets
salt and pepper
a large handful of fresh dill, chopped
a small handful of fresh parsley, roughly torn
4 spring onions, sliced
4 slices of lemon
4 small knobs of butter
seasonal green vegetables, to serve

`OTHER BEERS TO TRY`

Fourpure Pils Lager,
Sixpoint The Crisp,
Victory Prima Pils

`TRIED?`   `SCORE`

/10

`TASTING NOTES`

`EAT WITH BEER`

HOME-SMOKED MACKEREL & RODENBACH GRAND CRU

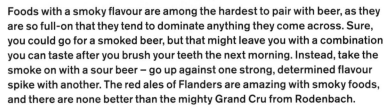

Smoke?... Think Tartness
Beer Style: Flanders Red

Foods with a smoky flavour are among the hardest to pair with beer, as they are so full-on that they tend to dominate anything they come across. Sure, you could go for a smoked beer, but that might leave you with a combination you can taste after you brush your teeth the next morning. Instead, take the smoke on with a sour beer – go up against one strong, determined flavour spike with another. The red ales of Flanders are amazing with smoky foods, and there are none better than the mighty Grand Cru from Rodenbach.

Open a bottle of Rodenbach's finest and make a mental note of what you smell emanating from the glass: the redcurrants and other sharp berry fruit. A slight vinegary tang. These are the vehicles that will help cut through and tame the smokiness – and the natural fattiness – of the mackerel. Grand Cru really is a hugely refreshing beer: a funky, tart, wine-like masterpiece of brewing that is at turns spicy, fruity and earthy. When tasted alone, Flanders reds can be overpowering at first – but when drunk with powerful foods, they are tempered and show their sweeter, fruitier side.

Smoking your own fish – or anything else – at home can be hugely complicated, but to make a relatively easy go of it all you need is a wok and a window that you can open. If you have a sturdy steel wok you can smoke direct – although the flavour will become ingrained so that every stir-fry from then on will also taste smoky. A more practical option is to cover the inside of the wok with foil to minimize this (which you will definitely have to do if you have a black-coated wok). A small wire rack is needed for the fish to sit on, but the lid must still be able to close, unless you want to really alarm the neighbours.

You can cure the fish first by dry-rubbing it with the sugar, salt and lemon pepper and then leaving it in the fridge for a few hours – or just season with salt and pepper – it's entirely up to you.

There are two methods for generating the smoke: first, add sawdust or wood chips to the foiled wok, then top with the wire rack and cured fish. Second, if you haven't shaved anything off a piece of furniture recently, you can add 50g (1¾oz) of uncooked white rice and 50g (1¾oz) of loose-leaf tea (Earl Grey, jasmine or Lapsang Souchong work really well) and this will have a similar effect. Put on the lid, seal with foil and turn the heat on low.

The brown sugar rub will colour the fish as it smokes, and the foil seal ensures that your kitchen won't be too smoky. Watch for escaping wisps, though. Heat for 10 minutes on low, then turn off the heat and let it stand for the same amount of time.

Check that the fish is cooked through after removing the lid (probably close the kitchen door first), and serve with rice or vegetables. Taste some on its own before drinking the beer, as the flavour differences will be instantly apparent. The tart, fruity beer will clean your palate of the smoky, oily fattiness from the mackerel with each forkful.

SERVES 2

Ingredients:

2 mackerel fillets
2 tablespoons soft brown sugar
1 teaspoon rock salt
1 teaspoon lemon and black pepper seasoning (available from good supermarkets, or use freshly ground black pepper and ½ a teaspoon of lemon zest)
wood chips or white rice and tea
rice or vegetables, to serve

OTHER BEERS TO TRY

Verhaeghe Duchesse de Bourgogne, The Bruery Oude Tart

TRIED?   SCORE

/10

TASTING NOTES

CHICKEN WINGS & BREWDOG PUNK IPA

Fat?... Think Bitterness
Beer Style: India Pale Ale

Beer and wings is a pairing that can be found in bars the length and breadth of North America – yet many still serve their finger-lickin' wings with lager. We beg to differ; quick and greasy foods are best served with something more complex. Hop bitterness cuts through fat, cleaning the palate for the next bite, so with these easy-to-cook chicken wings look for the quintessential US craft beer style, the India pale ale. Our flagship Punk IPA has the bitterness to aid the demolition of as big a bucket of wings as you can find.

Pour a bottle of Punk IPA into a glass and make a mental note of the aromas that result. Tropical fruit, citrus and a hint of caramel sweetness – these are the three pillars that will deal with the richness of the chicken and make the perfect pairing!

SERVES 6
Ingredients:
1 tablespoon paprika
1 teaspoon salt
1 teaspoon black pepper
½ teaspoon chilli powder
1kg (2lb 4oz) chicken wings
1 large knob of butter
ketchup and mayonnaise, to serve

Wings can be done in several ways: dropping them into hot fat gets the job done quicker, but for best results, bake them in a hot oven; the circulating air will dry out the skin and make it seriously crispy (or, to raise the bar, mix equal parts flour and Punk IPA with an egg and a teaspoon of baking powder for the ultimate battered wings).

Preheat the oven to 200°C/400°F/gas mark 6 and mix the dry ingredients together in the largest clear plastic bag you can find. At this point you can sprinkle in pretty much whatever you like, to give different flavour wings – cayenne pepper, curry powder to raise the heat, or oregano, thyme and dried parsley for a herb crusting. Ras el hanout would give you amazing Moroccan-style wings; it really is between you and the contents of your spice rack. Heck, you can even make up your own secret blend and pre-load it into an empty jar for when the wings-craving (inevitably) strikes.

If you buy prepared wings, throw them into the bag and get coating. If you've got whole wings, you'll need to do a bit of prep. Cut them into their natural three sections: the tip, the centre chunk (the wingette) and the drumstick-like drumette. Take a hefty knife and carefully bash through the joints to separate the three parts – the latter two can go into the bag. The wingtips won't have as much meat on them, so are better suited for making stock with. Make sure all the pieces of chicken are evenly coated in the herb/spice mix and you're ready to go!

Put the butter on a chunky baking tray and let it melt in the oven for a moment – this will coat the wings and ensure that the dry covering they currently have won't just burn in the heat. Empty the bag of wings into the melted butter and toss so they are (a) covered, and (b) evenly spread. Then close the oven door and let them get to it for 20 minutes. Come back and turn them, then cook for another 20 minutes, until cooked through. Serve with ketchup and mayonnaise. The challenge then is not to start eating them before they have cooled so you can actually hold them. It's difficult, take it from us.

OTHER BEERS TO TRY

Dogfish Head 60 Minute IPA,
Founders Centennial IPA,
The Kernel IPA Amarillo

TRIED?   SCORE

/10

TASTING NOTES

ROAST PORK & FULLER'S ESB

`Roast?... Think Caramel`
`Beer Style: Brown Ale`

Meat and beer are perfect bedfellows, due to the similarity in flavours that results from a little-known moment of science. The Maillard reaction is the chemical process by which browning occurs, in a similar way to caramelization. It's why meat goes into the oven one colour and emerges another, and why barley grains go darker when heated during the malting process. As such, brown beer and brown meat are the perfect complementary food pairing – it's a scientific fact.

Reach for an ESB and open it up. First brewed in 1971, it looks like a mahogany sideboard in the glass; you know what it's going to taste like from the first glance. There's a deep flavour of toffee, offset by a sweetness from the caramel malt that is lifted by orange citrus from the hops. Everything about this beer screams "Sunday roast" – and with a roast pork dish you can balance the sweeter flavours and the malt-led roastiness perfectly. And if you have two bottles, halve the amount of stock and replace with beer instead for a richer gravy.

Roast pork is a classic "pay it forward" dish – the hard work starts when the oven goes on and ends when the tray goes in. After that it's just the waiting game, although you can use this time to prepare vegetable accompaniments, knock up a sticky toffee pudding, or just see how many beers you need to fully appreciate the flavours. Anyway, pork shoulder is best for this dish; other cuts are fine but shoulder works amazingly well – boned makes things easier, but if you are a whiz with a knife and are saving the beer for later, a bone-in shoulder gives even more flavour.

Preheat the oven to 180°C/350°F/gas mark 4. Put the salt, pepper, marjoram, cumin, mustard seeds, paprika and garlic into a pestle and mortar and smash to a paste, then spread this paste over the fatty upper layer of the pork (for best results, score it with a knife first).

In a hot, oiled pan, sear the seasoned joint for a few minutes, until the fat starts to brown – Maillard at work – and the kitchen fills with the smells of garlic and spices. Take the pork off the heat, put it into a casserole dish and add the vegetables and three-quarters of the stock.

Cover the dish with foil and place in the oven for 1 hour 20 minutes. After an hour of this time, check and baste with the remaining stock if the dish is looking a little dry. Once cooked, take the meat out and let it rest. Sieve the juices into a pan and bring to the boil. Add the flour to thicken (or beef gravy mix to dial the flavour up a notch), then slice the pork, pour over the gravy and serve with vegetables, mashed potatoes or anything else that takes your fancy.

SERVES 4

Ingredients:

1 teaspoon salt
1 teaspoon cracked black pepper
1 teaspoon dried marjoram
1 teaspoon cumin seeds
1 teaspoon mustard seeds
1 teaspoon paprika
2 garlic cloves
2kg (4lb 8oz) pork shoulder
2 small onions, diced
2 small carrots, diced
1 litre (34fl oz) beef stock
1 tablespoon plain white flour

TRIED?   SCORE

/10

TASTING NOTES

ROASTED MUSHROOM AND TOMATO PIZZA & AECHT SCHLENKERLA RAUCHBIER

Umami?... Think smoky
Beer Style: Rauchbier

Beer and pizza is about as good as it gets. Unless you make the pizza yourself and pair it with a smoked beer, that is. The savouriness of umami is lifted by the classic Rauchbier – the tomatoes, the earthy mushrooms – and also the parts of the pizza you maybe didn't intend. Blackened pizza crust is an exact match for smoked beer, the dark char and the smoky beer going brilliantly together. And if you happen to have a wood-fired pizza oven in your garden, then you'll be able to marry those flavours even more.

As we said on page 110, Rauchbiers are the among the most challenging beer styles you can encounter. That first hit of liquid bacon takes some getting used to – but for those new to their mysteries, the best way to get an appreciation of their flavour is to start off by pairing them with food; a culinary introduction helps give these flavours some context. The beech-smoked malt that forms the backbone of the beer is mirrored in the similar heat-induced elements of the pizza – so as you uncap Bamberg's finest export and wonder why beer would taste that way, let Italy's finest export guide your hand.

Find a large bowl and add the flour, yeast and salt – you can sieve the flour first if you like, but modern flours are finely ground as it is, so you should be fine just carefully pouring it from the bag. Make a fist-sized hole in the middle of the flour and add the olive oil and a dribble of the water. Work those forearms by slowly combining the liquid into the dusty flour and making the whole thing into a thick paste. Over time, as you add the water in stages, the dough will start to come together. At this stage you can add more flour if the mass is too gloopy, or more water if it's too solid.

Finish by mixing with your hands, kneading the dough so it becomes more elastic to the touch. Place in a bowl (the same one if you've been able to wash it up in between) and cover with a cloth. Leave to rise for an hour.

Meanwhile, preheat the oven to 230°C/450°F/gas mark 8.

Once the doughball has grown in size, tip it out onto a floured board and push with the heel of your hand outwards from the centre. Move around in a circle, until the ball has become a base, and the pizza-to-be has thinned out to about 5mm (¼ inch). Top with passata, mushrooms, cheese (it's a pizza, you know the drill) and cook in the oven for 10 minutes.

MAKES 1 X 30CM (12 INCH) PIZZA

Ingredients:

170g (6oz) plain white flour
1 teaspoon dried yeast
¼ teaspoon salt
1 tablespoon olive oil
120ml (4fl oz) hot water
2 tablespoons passata
75g (2½oz) chestnut mushrooms, sliced
1 ball of buffalo mozzarella
fresh basil, finely chopped

OTHER BEERS TO TRY

Beavertown Smog Rocket Smoked Porter,
Alaskan Smoked Porter,
Mikkeller Beer Geek Bacon

TRIED?   **SCORE**

          /10

TASTING NOTES

POTATO & PEA CURRY
& WESTMALLE TRAPPIST DUBBEL

Heat?... Think Malt
Beer Style: Belgian Trappist Dubbel

As we noted earlier, the heat of Indian food and the hops of IPA act to emphasize each other – which is totally fine if you have a cast-iron constitution and an immunity to chilli. But for a more beneficial curry pairing, the sweeter, more malt-forward beers are the way to go – and a Belgian Trappist dubbel is the ideal marker for the heat of a classic aloo matar. With this recipe, there's a second-level matching in the form of the earthy potatoes meeting the bready malt as well ...

The mightily named Abdij Onze-Lieve-Vrouw van het Heilig Hart van Jezus was founded in 1794 northeast of Antwerp – and although they popularized the tripel style in the 1930s, Westmalle Trappist dubbel is also world-class, and equally deserving of praise. With its dark fruit, esters and spicy phenols, it has a wide range of flavours that act to warm you up on a cold day while also being a great foil for spicy food. The pepperiness lifts the earthy notes of the curry, and the rich dark, fruit acts to put a ceiling on the chilli. Belgians – not known for their curries – have inadvertently created the perfect pairing for them.

While you're enjoying the initial flavours of the Trappist dubbel, heat the oil in a large pan and sauté the onion until it is soft and translucent. Add the garlic and ginger and cook for a short time, being careful not to let them burn. Next, add all the dried spices and stir into an aromatic oniony paste – the smells that fill your kitchen will be hard to resist at this point. Now add the potatoes. Make sure that the spices cover all the faces of the diced spuds, then add the chopped tomatoes and the stock, give it an almighty stir and put on the lid.

Simmer for as long as you can stand – at least half an hour, but check the potatoes and if they need longer you can add more stock or water. If they are done before then, and the curry is too runny, you can add a little cornflour and stir to thicken. However, every side dish from the Indian subcontinent is designed to soak up sauces – so your rice or naan that will go alongside will help you out in this regard. As long as the potatoes are cooked, you can call it whenever you like.

Add the peas a few minutes before the end, and the fresh herbs just prior to serving. Enjoy with the Trappist dubbel, and discover a new side to curries.

SERVES 4

Ingredients:

1 tablespoon vegetable oil
1 onion, chopped
2 garlic cloves, chopped
a thumb-sized piece of ginger, grated
1 teaspoon ground cumin
½ teaspoon chilli powder
½ teaspoon ground coriander
½ teaspoon garam masala
¼ teaspoon turmeric
2 large potatoes, cut into 1cm
  (½ inch) cubes
1 x 400g (14oz) tin of chopped
  tomatoes
300ml (10fl oz) vegetable stock
cornflour, to thicken (optional)
200g (7oz) frozen peas
a small bunch of fresh coriander
  leaves, chopped
basmati rice and naan bread, to serve

OTHER BEERS TO TRY

Chimay Rouge Pères Trappistes,
Affligem Dubbel,
Trappistes Rochefort 6

TRIED?   **SCORE**

     /10

TASTING NOTES

CHOCOLATE TORTE & BROOKLYN BLACK CHOCOLATE STOUT

EAT WITH BEER

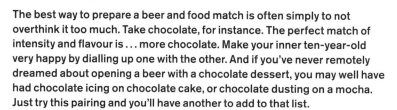

Chocolate?... Think Cacao
Beer Style: Imperial Stout

The best way to prepare a beer and food match is often simply to not overthink it too much. Take chocolate, for instance. The perfect match of intensity and flavour is . . . more chocolate. Make your inner ten-year-old very happy by dialling up one with the other. And if you've never remotely dreamed about opening a beer with a chocolate dessert, you may well have had chocolate icing on chocolate cake, or chocolate dusting on a mocha. Just try this pairing and you'll have another to add to that list.

Imperial stout is a beer style that is just crying out for a bit of food-based recognition. Perfect armchair sippers, they come into their own when added alongside a chocolatey dessert. The best straight-up examples (i.e. not those that have been added to ex-whisky barrels) taste like liquid chocolate anyway – and right at the top of the tree is this jaw-dropping stout from Brooklyn Brewery. Rolling in at an even 10.0% ABV, it is a thing of beauty in the glass and should be enjoyed as close to room temperature as you can get it, to open up the aromas and flavours to their fullest extent. Rich, resonant imperial stouts like this one are best matched with a dark, slightly bitter dessert such as this torte (even we agree it is possible to have too much of a good thing).

Preheat the oven to 160°C/320°F/gas mark 3, and grease and line the sides of a 25cm (10 inch) loose-bottomed round cake tin – there is nothing worse than that moment of glory ebbing into the disappointment of a stuck torte, pulling away from the tin in pieces.

Put the chocolate and butter into a small pan and melt until smooth – it helps if the butter isn't straight out of the fridge.

Meanwhile, using an electric whisk (powered by electricity) or a hand whisk (powered by the first few sips of Black Chocolate Stout), beat the eggs and sugar together for 5 minutes until the mixture is the consistency of thick, pale custard. You'll see it come together before your eyes, so when it's just there, pour the now-cooled chocolate and butter mix into the whisked egg and sugar, and fold it in very carefully using a large metal spoon. The aim here is to let everything mingle together without knocking the air out of it, so use gentle carving motions with the spoon until all before you is the same colour.

In a separate small bowl, combine the flour, almonds and the salt and then keep the forearm workout going by folding this into your mix as well. Ensure everything is blended together and still light and full of air, then spoon into the greased cake tin and allow to settle to an even height all the way around. Bake for 35–40 minutes, until evenly set with a slight crust all over the top – and crucially leave to cool before releasing from the tin.

Dust with cocoa or icing sugar (your choice) and cut as generous a slice as you feel you have earned (hand-whiskers deserve more). . .

MAKES 1 LARGE TORTE

Ingredients:

300g (10½oz) 70% dark chocolate, broken up
300g (10½oz) unsalted butter
6 large eggs
300g (10½oz) golden caster sugar
75g (2½oz) plain white flour
75g (2½oz) ground almonds
¼ teaspoon salt
cocoa powder or icing sugar, for dusting

OTHER BEERS TO TRY

Oskar Blues Ten Fidy,
Great Divide Yeti,
Dieu du Ciel! Péché Mortel

TRIED?   SCORE

/10

TASTING NOTES

APPLE PIE & ANCHOR PORTER

EAT WITH BEER

Sweet?... Think Roasty
Beer Style: Porter

The "pie and a pint" stereotype may be limited to the meat side of the pastry divide, but beer can also pair fantastically well with fruit fillings. Take dark beer – it isn't just a natural bedfellow with steak pie, the roasty, caramel and stone-fruit elements serve to balance the sweetness of a homely apple pie. Many nations enjoy that particular dessert, but in this case we are looking over the Atlantic for a classic apple pie, so we can pair it with another classic from the United States – Anchor Porter.

Anchor are world-famous for their Steam Beer – which would be another great match for apple pie – but the sweeter the dish, the roastier the beer should be to offset. Hence the porter, which pours black as pitch and with dark aromas to match. Coffee, chocolate, dark fruit, caramel – first brewed in 1972, this is truly a fantastic beer, and has flavours that are nuanced and play out across several levels. The deepness of the roast from the black and chocolate malts, and the darkly fruity Northern Brewer hops all balance the sweet, sugary hit from the apple sauce and the butteriness of the pastry.

Preheat the oven to 200°C/400°F/gas mark 6.

Sieve the flour, sugar, cornflour and salt into a bowl, then rub in the butter until the mixture resembles fine breadcrumbs. Add the egg to the flour mixture, then, using a small knife, mix the egg into the flour, using your hand to firm up the mixture. The pastry should be of an even colour and a suitable consistency for rolling. Divide into two halves, then roll out one half on a lightly floured board so that it is big enough to cover a 20cm (8 inch) enamel or aluminium pie dish. Trim the edges with a knife, using the edge of the plate as your guide.

Cover the pastry with the stewed apples and sprinkle with sugar to taste. Now you can work on the lid – the destiny for the other half of the pastry. Roll it out, moisten the edge of the bottom layer of pastry and place this newly rolled piece on top. Press down on the pastry edges, making sure they are properly sealed. Trim off any excess pastry with a knife, again using the plate as your guide. Flute the edges with a pinching action, using your fingers and thumb to make it look even more awesome.

Prick the surface of the pastry lightly and place the pie in the oven. Bake for 20–30 minutes, and dust with sugar before serving with custard.

MAKES 1 LARGE PIE

Ingredients:

330g (11½oz) plain white flour
150g (5½oz) caster sugar
25g (1oz) cornflour
½ teaspoon salt
200g (7oz) unsalted butter
1 egg, beaten

For the filling
3 large Bramley cooking apples,
   chopped, stewed and cooled
sugar, to taste

caster sugar, to serve
custard, to serve

OTHER BEERS TO TRY

Fuller's London Porter,
Tempest Red Eye Flight,
Rogue Mocha Porter

TRIED?   SCORE

/10

TASTING NOTES

KINGPIN

LAGER REBORN

You only need to conduct a brief round of mental word association for "lager" and the first things that pop into the grey matter are images of ice-cold suds from expensive advertising campaigns. It is one of the scandals of the brewing world that the history and innovation of this style have been shunted aside by the lowest common denominator: beer making on an industrial scale.

So Kingpin is our attempt to redress the balance.

We channelled the spirit of classic German Pilsners (and our German brewer Franz) into a king among knaves – a true 21st-century lager. Kingpin is the latest in our family of cold-conditioned beers to act as a barrier to the worldwide stream of mass-produced insipidness. If you think lagers taste of nothing, then think again. Frozen tankards need not apply.

Brewed with 100% malted barley, Kingpin is lager reborn and a nail in the coffin of other beers that rely on flashy adverts or gimmicks to reach their audience. Call us crazy, but we believe the taste of the beer should always be the most important factor, so we don't bulk our recipe out with cheaper ingredients such as rice or maize (as other, larger producers of this formative style do).

This full-bodied malt character acts as a base upon which to layer the hop-load, setting the bar for everything that follows. As a showcase for the quintessential German one-two of floral notes and spicy hop bitterness, we are proud of Kingpin's classically assertive roots. It is the majesty of German beer in a nutshell – nothing extra, nothing unnecessary.

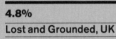

like that?
try these:

TIPOPILS
5.2%
Birrificio Italiano, Italy

Dry and hoppy, the world's best unknown lager

KELLER PILS
4.8%
Lost and Grounded, UK

Crisp, dry and bready with bitterness and refreshment in equal quantity

PRIMA PILS
5.3%
Victory Brewing Co, USA

Lemon zest in abundance in the quintessential US Pils

21ST CENTURY LAGER

RELEASED	2016
ABV	4.7%
STYLE	LAGER
IBU	40
HOPS	MAGNUM, PERLE, PERLA
MALT	PILSNER, PALE, CARA, MUNICH

"WE'VE BEEN WORKING ON THE PROFILE OF OUR YEASTS SO THAT WE CAN DELIVER THE AROMAS AND FLAVOURS OF A FULLY AUTHENTIC GERMAN-STYLE PILSNER – AND KINGPIN IS THE RESULT."
— BREWDOG BREWER FRANZ HORAK

"KINGPIN IS THE PERFECT INTRODUCTION TO CRAFT BEER AWAY FROM MAINSTREAM BLANDNESS. IT OPENS UP YOUR TASTE BUDS INTO A WORLD OF (H)OPPORTUNITY."
— EQUITY PUNK ALAN MOCHRIE

DROPTICK
TICK THIS BEER OFF YOUR LIST WITH A DROP FROM YOUR FINGER

YOU SAY:

....
....
....
....
....
....
....
....

Beer is a natural accompaniment to food – but it also has a long and rich heritage of being used in food – as an ingredient. From *la cuisine à la bière* in Belgium to the modern-day US brewhouse taprooms adding beer to the daily specials, beer can add a depth of flavour to dozens of dishes. It's not a waste; it's an elevation of the work of the brewers. Here are ten cases in point.

IPA & CITRUS SALAD

Beer: Stone Ruination IPA
Style: Double IPA

Foods traditionally enjoyed with beer tend to be the hearty, emphatic, filling variety – very few people watch the clock edge towards 5pm and rise from their desk with a "Let's go for beers and salad!" But the preponderance of citrus-forward pale ales these days actually makes a very good pairing for bitter leafy greens with zesty dressings – and in this case, you can make the beer a central component of the whole shebang by including it in the dressing. Find a couple of bottles of double IPA and go for it.

Like everything else they do, Stone's double IPA is upfront, in your face, and uncompromising (and that's just the label). Open one of the bottles or cans and pour into a clean glass – the aromas will hopefully remind you of things that would go well with salad leaves: heavy citrus, floral notes and then a finish of sticky resin. This is a fantastic beer, and one that will elevate the humble vinaigrette to new heights. For the recipe, you'll need to keep back about 4 tablespoons, so, lucky you, there'll be plenty of that second bottle left over as well. Either make a larger batch of dressing for the fridge, or . . . y'know . . .

Open one of the bottles of Stone Ruination and pour about 4 tablespoons into a small bowl. Add the vinegar and mustard and mix with a small whisk (or a very fast fork). Add the lemon and orange zest, salt and pepper and continue to blend – the dressing may have a beer-like head at this point.

Slowly mix in the oil, which will give the dressing more body and help to calm things down a little. Then all you need do is pour it liberally over the salad leaves and enjoy with the rest of the beer!

You can add chicken or fish to make more of a main meal of it, or add chilli, spring onions, basil or honey to the dressing to change the flavours slightly. Or try a kriek instead of the double IPA . . .

SERVES 2 AS A SIDE

Ingredients:

2 bottles of Stone Ruination IPA
1 tablespoon balsamic vinegar
1 tablespoon wholegrain mustard
zest of ½ a lemon
zest of ½ an orange
salt and pepper
1 tablespoon olive oil
110g (4oz) mixed bitter salad leaves
   (such as rocket, endive, spinach
   and watercress)
cooked chicken or fish, to serve
   (optional)

OTHER BEERS TO TRY

Moor JJJ,
Magic Rock Human Cannonball,
Dogfish Head 90 Minute Imperial IPA

TRIED?   SCORE

                /10

TASTING NOTES

BEAN BURGER

Beer: Thornbridge Wild Raven
Style: Stout

COOK WITH BEER

Beer and a burger is a universal delight, but beer in a burger will likely be a new experience for even the most regular bun-fiend. For those that avoid meat, their options can sometimes fall apart in the excitement, or be unfairly dry – so the addition of our favourite beverage in the mix helps bind everything together as well as delivering an improved taste. Stout is a natural partner to a bean burger – both have dark, earthy flavours and the beer permeates to the heart of what could very well be your favourite new burger option. For added flavour, grill on an outdoor barbecue and serve with potato and chive salad.

Black IPA is the classic oxymoron of brewing – that something can be both black and pale at the same time – but in practice what results is a true "best of both worlds" in your glass. Like a hoppy stout, the beer has a baseline of deep, roasty chocolate before a whack of citrus, resin or tropical fruit. Truly a beer in transition, black IPAs deliver a fascinating realization of the individual impact of malt and hops on flavour, and how they can complement each other. They are reasonably common now, but one of the best originates from the UK's Peak District – the sublime Thornbridge Wild Raven – and it really lifts a bean burger.

MAKES 6 BURGERS

Ingredients:

2 bottles of Thornbridge Wild Raven
1 tablespoon vegetable oil
1 red onion, diced
2 garlic cloves, diced
2 x 400g (14oz) tins of mixed beans, drained
1 small tin (about 200g/7oz) of sweetcorn, drained
1 teaspoon cayenne pepper
1 teaspoon ground cumin
50g (1¾oz) chickpea flour or plain white flour
burger buns, salad and condiments, to serve

Open one of the bottles, pour 100ml (3½fl oz) into a glass, and set aside.

In a small pan, heat the oil and fry the onion and garlic until they are translucent and cooked, then remove from the heat and allow to cool.

The next step depends – if it's not too personal a question – on how chunky you like your burgers. You can either mix the rest of the ingredients in a bowl, mashing the beans and sweetcorn with a fork to break them up but leave them fairly solid, or you can blitz everything together in a food processor to give a smoother – but equally pliable – paste. It really is down to your own personal preference. Bean burgers with a larger surface area take longer to cook, but how they look is up to you.

However you decide to mix the ingredients, combine the beans, sweetcorn, cooled onion and garlic and the spices and get everything well integrated. Add the glass of beer and you'll have quite a wet paste, which is where the flour comes in. Add this in stages, blending as you go, until the mixture is one you can pick up and form into burgers. You can use chickpea flour if you have it, which will give a slightly deeper, earthier flavour – but plain white flour is fine. Divide the mix into as many burgers as you think you can eat (they freeze pretty well too), then grill, fry or add to your barbecue until browned on both sides and cooked through. Serve in burger buns with crispy salad and your favourite condiments. Perfect.

OTHER BEERS TO TRY

Buxton Imperial Black,
Beavertown Black Betty,
21st Amendment Back in Black

TRIED?   SCORE

/10

TASTING NOTES

MÄRZEN & MAC 'N' CHEESE

Beer: Weihenstephaner Oktoberfestbier
Style: Märzen

Seriously, don't knock this until you've tried it. As anyone who's ever had mac 'n' cheese knows, it has a one-dimensional flavour (which is what makes it one of the most amazing comfort foods). From the first spoonful to the last, it doesn't vary. The addition of a deep amber beer – like the classic seasonal lagers of Germany – adds a toasty, bready element to this flavour. It leads the whole thing into a mac 'n' cheese on toast direction, which is something quite wonderful. The esteemed festival brewers of Munich may not have had this in mind when they created the style, but it can be our little secret.

Time to convert your kitchen into a Bierkeller. Open up a bottle of Oktoberfest – the original beers served at the iconic Munich beer celebration (since the 1990s anyone lucky enough to attend would have been drinking the lighter-coloured Festbiers). The bready, toasty beer is brewed with a single thing in mind – en masse consumption – so the hops only exist to balance the sweetness. Munich malt yields a complex maltiness that makes Oktoberfest the perfect long-distance beer; it gives you just enough to keep you interested but not too much to overpower. It is, in a word, comforting.

Open one of the bottles of Weihenstephan's finest and pour 250ml (9fl oz) into a glass.

In a chunky pot on the stove, melt the butter and gently heat the garlic through. Pour in the glass of beer, then add the milk and heat until it starts to have regular bubbles break the surface. To this pale soup add the macaroni and stir well, then keep on simmering for 15–20 minutes, until the sauce has reduced and the pasta has cooked (or more accurately, poached).

You can either keep the mac 'n' cheese in the big dish (to enjoy all to yourself) or decant into smaller serving dishes at this point. Add the cheese and don't stir it in too much; if you then put the dish (or dishes) under the grill you will get a crispy melted topping that will be brown and crunchy on top and perfectly soft and gooey underneath.

SERVES 4

Ingredients:

2 bottles of Weihenstephaner
  Oktoberfestbier
50g (1¾oz) butter
1 garlic clove, diced
500ml (18fl oz) semi-skimmed milk
250g (9oz) macaroni
150g (5½oz) Cheddar cheese,
  grated
150g (5½oz) Parmesan cheese,
  grated

OTHER BEERS TO TRY

Hacker-Pschorr Original Oktoberfest,
Augustiner Bräu Oktoberfest,
Samuel Adams Octoberfest

TRIED?   SCORE

                /10

TASTING NOTES

THAI-STYLE PRAWN CAKES & SALAD

COOK WITH BEER

```
Beer: Boon Oude Geuze
Style: Lambic
```

This one is firmly parked under the bracket marked "fusion", with very little chance of the spicy, chilli-laden fishcakes of the East meeting the dry, puckering, spontaneously fermented beers of Belgium in the wild. But why not combine the two? Lambic offers a touch of bitterness, tartness and acidity that can help bring this classic Thai staple together – and with such a riot of flavours going on, the beer adds a background hum and depth that helps combat the enormous chilli heat (if you push the boat out and add the smallest, angriest-looking chillies you can find, that is).

Frank Boon has been making this beer the same way since 1975, and it has an inescapable aroma of grapefruit, grapes, ginger and oaky wood from the enormous *foudres* (casks) the beer is aged in at the Boon brewery in the small town of Lembeek (the town that gave name to the style). Geuze (or Gueuze in the alternative spelling) are different aged lambics, and Boon are masters of the art of blending.

Uncork the beer, pointing away from treasured items of pottery or family members, and pour into a small glass. The beer will instantly froth upwards, eager to escape. You'll need 125ml (4fl oz) for this recipe, so set that aside in a small glass – the rest is fair game.

Put the beans (you can use peas if edamame are hard to source), onion, chilli, garlic, lime leaves and lemongrass into a food processor and blitz into a paste. Add the fish and prawns and whiz up again, but for less time, leaving a few small chunks of meat remaining. Then add the liquids – the beer, the egg and the oyster sauce – and pulse until everything is combined into a consistency you can form small patties out of. This is the next step – so wet your hands and press the mixture into 5cm (2 inch) wide discs. Letting them cool a little in the fridge will help maintain the shape while frying, or you can keep them overnight.

Heat some oil in a pan and shallow-fry the prawn cakes until golden-brown on both sides, transfer to kitchen paper to soak up the excess oil. Serve with rice, chilli sauce or even the salad and citrus IPA dressing on page 197. The lambic will be perceptible (depending on how strong the chillies are) as a tart, vinegary umami-ness and the remaining beer will go really well with the fiery, savoury sweetness.

SERVES 4

Ingredients:

2 bottles of Boon Oude Geuze
50g (1¾oz) edamame beans, shelled
1 red onion, chopped
2 red chillies, chopped
2 garlic cloves, chopped
2 kaffir lime leaves
½ a stalk of lemongrass, chopped
200g (7oz) white fish (haddock will do)
200g (7oz) peeled jumbo prawns
1 egg
1 tablespoon oyster sauce
1 tablespoon groundnut oil, for frying
chilli sauce, to serve

OTHER BEERS TO TRY

Cantillon Lou Pepe,
3 Fonteinen Oude Geuze,
Lindemans Cuvée René

TRIED?　　**SCORE**

/10

TASTING NOTES

MUSSELS IN GOSE

Beer: Magic Rock Salty Kiss
Style: Gose

Cooking seafood can be a tricky prospect; many denizens of the deep have a tiny window of perfection in between being raw or ruined. Miss that window, and their delicate flavours and textures will be long gone. So go for mussels – they take on a range of flavours amazingly well and are done the moment their shells open. All you need to do is keep an eye on them. Mussels steamed in beer is one of the all-time classic beer recipes, and it is just so easy to cook. Classically steamed in witbier, for an extra kick of savoury brininess, switch up the beer for one of the styles of the moment: the floral, salty Gose.

The aromas of the beer should immediately transport you to the nearest coastline – ozone from the salt alongside the sharpness of sea buckthorn and gooseberry. The addition of fruit to the classic salty/sour wheat beer adds another layer and makes for a hugely refreshing beer – one that will work its way brilliantly into the natural salty, earthy nature of the mussels.

Open one of the cans and pour the beer into a clean glass. While sipping, scrub the mussels under cold running water if they have any stringy beards still attached, and throw away any that are open if they don't immediately close when tapped.

In a large deep pan – a wok is pretty good for this if you aren't busy smoking something in it (although smoked mussels are also incredible) – fry the shallots and garlic in a little oil or butter and then add the mussels. Get them coated in the oily goodness, then slowly pour in the second can of Salty Kiss. Another stir and put a lid on the pan, giving an occasional gentle shake to keep things moving. After 5 minutes take off the lid, dodge the roiling ball of steam (albeit taking in some of the aroma) and check the shells. If they are all open then you're good to go – although it may take another couple of minutes.

Discard any mussels that have resolutely stayed closed, then add the parsley and give a squeeze of lemon over the top. Ladle into a deep bowl and serve with a hunk of crusty bread on the side. The flavours of the beer – in particular the sharper fruit flavours and the floral notes from the hops – will hopefully have penetrated the mussels, and the reduced beer will have been enhanced by the liquor emerging from within the shells.

SERVES 2

Ingredients:

2 cans of Magic Rock Salty Kiss
800g (1lb 12oz) mussels
2 shallots, sliced
1 garlic clove, diced
a little oil or butter
1 small bunch of fresh flat-leaf
  parsley, roughly torn
lemon wedges and crusty bread,
  to serve

OTHER BEERS TO TRY

Westbrook Gose,
Modern Times Fruitlands, Cigar
City Gose

TRIED?   SCORE

                /10

TASTING NOTES

BEER-BATTERED COD

Beer: BrewDog Dead Pony Club
Style: Pale Ale

This is arguably the most tried-and-tested recipe featuring beer in existence. Adding a splash of beer to a batter isn't just a great way to showcase beer – it is almost a prerequisite for your crispy coating to have a decent flavour. Unless you're one of those people who use sparkling water. For everyone else, our session pale ale Dead Pony Club is a fantastic addition to a batter, as the citrus from the hops gives a lemony boost to the white fish and the pale ale malt bill increases the savoury bite of the batter. And once cooked to perfection, the beer itself then goes perfectly with the result – it's karma, in battered form.

When you open a bottle the toasted malt aromas give way to tropical fruit, citrus and floral notes, and on the taste these come across in a similar fashion: the pithy fruit following on from the biscuity baseline. You can discover more about our session pale ale on page 83, but in a nutshell this is our go-to beer, one that delivers refreshment, citrus and balance but at a strength you can return to again and again. And every now and again we love nothing more than to sacrifice a cupful to an ultimate fate – becoming part of Britain's favourite national dish.

Flip the cap off a bottle of Dead Pony – or open a can – and pour yourself a glass. You're going to need 250ml (9fl oz) of beer for the batter, so set that aside.

Sieve the flour into a large bowl to begin the aeration (the more air you get into your batter, the lighter it will be). Add the oil and begin whisking with a hand whisk or an electric mixer on its lowest setting. As the oil starts to pull the flour into a ragged ball, start to add the beer a splash at a time. The stop-start inclusion of the beer stops it foaming everywhere and also gives the flour time to absorb the liquid evenly without creating lumps (which you are also busy whisking out). Once all in, you want a consistency that will run slowly from the back of a spoon. Then chill the batter for an hour.

Heat a deep pan of oil and dunk the fish in the batter, ensuring it's totally covered and that as much loose batter has run off as possible. Carefully lower the fish into the oil, letting it fall away from you so as not to splash, and fry for 5 minutes, until golden. Remove and allow to drain on kitchen paper to remove the excess fat, then serve with chips, mushy peas, angry seagulls overhead and the other bottle (or can) of Dead Pony Club.

SERVES 2
Ingredients:

2 bottles of BrewDog Dead Pony Club
200g (7oz) plain white flour
1 tablespoon vegetable oil
oil, for deep frying
2 fillets of white fish (cod, haddock, whiting, pollock)
chips and mushy peas, to serve
salt and pepper (optional)

OTHER BEERS TO TRY

Stone Go To IPA,
Firestone Walker Easy Jack,
Brew By Numbers Session IPA

TRIED?　　SCORE

/10

TASTING NOTES

TWICE SMOKY CHILLI

Beer: Beavertown Smog Rocket
Style: Smoked Porter

There are a few ways you can transform a chilli into one worthy of the hardiest range-crossing cowboy. One is to add as much smoked paprika as you dare. Another is to add a smoked beer into the equation. So this one has both. Beavertown's Smog Rocket uses nine different malts in the brewing process, with the German Rauchmalt acting as the perfect complement to the paprika in this recipe. Both of these elements work really well with the beef, cumin and tomato flavours, and when the whole thing is reduced very, very slowly you're left with the best – and smokiest – chilli anywhere. Campfire-tastic.

This one is all about low and slow; taking the ethos behind American barbecue and turning it to the humble chilli con carne. But before that, we have a beer to sample. Beavertown's epic smoked porter was inspired by London's industrial revolution and has the aromas of a busy city on the move – lots of smoke from the German malt and sweeter, darker notes of stone fruit and dried raisins. On the taste, these elements kick off the flavour profile, but the smoke builds and rises to win through on the finish – it really is a fantastic beer, and as we'll see is a brilliant option to add a smoky depth to a chilli.

Heat the oil in a chunky pan. Slowly fry the onion until translucent, then add the garlic and cook for a little longer. Add the minced beef and break it apart, turning it in the oil until it has all changed colour from red to brown. You can even let it get a little darker at this stage – any further colour will come out as another seam of smokiness in the final dish (just be careful not to burn the garlic). This will probably take about 10 minutes.

Now add the dried spices and give everything a good stir. Move the spicy beef around for a couple of minutes to ensure all the meat has been covered in the spice. Add the tomatoes and 1 can of Smog Rocket, stirring to loosen anything that has stuck to the bottom of the pan. Add the tomato purée and blend it into the sauce, throw in the bay leaf, then deposit the kidney beans in as well.

Give everything a further stir and put the lid on, then turn the heat to as low as it will go and still keep it quietly bubbling, and simmer for 30 minutes. Check it after 10 and then 20 to make sure it's not sticking too much (it will to some degree) and move things around. This is the time to cook some rice to go alongside or open a pack of tortilla chips (or both). Then serve with chopped avocado, sour cream, coriander, tortilla chips and the second can of Smog Rocket!

SERVES 4

Ingredients:

1 tablespoon vegetable oil
1 large onion, diced
2 garlic cloves, diced
500g (1lb 2oz) beef mince
1 teaspoon smoked paprika
1 teaspoon ground cumin
½ teaspoon cayenne pepper
1 x 400g (14oz) tin of chopped
  tomatoes
2 cans of Beavertown Smog Rocket
1 tablespoon tomato purée
1 bay leaf
1 x 400g (14oz) tin of red kidney
  beans, drained
chopped avocado, sour cream,
  coriander leaves and tortilla chips,
  to serve

OTHER BEERS TO TRY

Stone Smoked Porter,
Aecht Schlenkerla Eiche Doppelbock,
Left Hand Smoke Jumper

TRIED?   SCORE

                /10

TASTING NOTES

FLANDERS-STYLE BRAISED RABBIT

Beer: Liefmans Goudenband
Style: Oud Bruin

You don't need to speak Flemish to take a flying stab at the translation for this style. The old brown ales of Flanders date back over 400 years, and were designed to mature and develop over time. This makes them fantastic beers to age, but also seems to make them worthy additions to stews, roasts and casseroles – anything that also takes a while to come together. Oud Bruins can't be rushed, and neither can this classic Belgian recipe. The fruity sourness permeates the meat and seasons it as the stew cooks; plus the slight tartness it has offsets the richness of the reduced sauce ...

The most complex beer produced by the Liefman's brewery, their "gold band" is a massive beer in every respect. Pour yourself a glass and indulge in the aromas. Raisins and berry fruit, a slight tingle of sharpness, set amid a backdrop of sweeter caramel malt – this is one of those beers that deliver something different with every sip. It is intense, but really well balanced – a true mark of great Belgian brewing. And like many from that country, it adds depth and character to a rustic stew. So let's concentrate on that for the immediate future. Glass down!

Open one of the bottles of Goudenband, pour 100ml (3½fl oz) into a glass, and set it aside. Preheat the oven to 160°C/320°F/gas mark 3.

Coat the rabbit in seasoned flour, then heat some butter in a chunky casserole dish over a medium heat. Add the rabbit and brown on all sides, sealing in the flavour, then remove and add a splash of oil to the encrusted pan. Free up the bottom – releasing those charred parts – then add the onion, carrot, celery and mushrooms. Fry for 5 minutes, until the vegetables are starting to soften, then add the garlic and do the same. After a few minutes, add the glass of beer and the chicken stock, give everything a really good stir, and tuck the rabbit under the surface. Put the thyme, bay leaf and parsley on top.

Put the lid on the casserole and cook in the oven for 1½ hours, stirring occasionally to stop things sticking together. After an hour, check the thickness of the sauce and add more stock or beer (if you can spare the beer) if the stew is looking a little too chunky. Once the rabbit is cooked through, remove the dish from the oven, ladle into bowls, top with parsley and serve with some crusty bread and the rest of the thunderous Oud Bruin.

The tart, dark, sweet and sour nature of the beer will go really well with the gamey, earthy and slightly rich-tasting rabbit.

SERVES 2

Ingredients:

2 bottles of Liefmans Goudenband
1 rabbit, cut into large chunks
80g (3oz) plain flour
salt and pepper
a little butter
1 onion, diced
1 large carrot, diced
1 stick of celery, diced
200g (7oz) chestnut mushrooms, halved
2 garlic cloves, diced
125ml (4fl oz) chicken stock
1 sprig of fresh thyme
1 bay leaf
1 small handful of fresh parsley, chopped
crusty bread, to serve

OTHER BEERS TO TRY

Petrus Oud Bruin,
New Belgium La Folie,
Ommegang Rosetta

TRIED?   SCORE

/10

TASTING NOTES

JELLY & ICE CREAM

Beer: Lindemans Framboise
Style: Framboise

OK, so this isn't exactly breaking the culinary bank. But even Michelin-starred chefs eat jelly and ice cream. Adding alcohol isn't just to move away from the children's party feel and lend the wobbles some degree of respectability; it also adds flavour! So forget vodka jelly in Magaluf and embrace beer jelly, made with classic Belgian fruit beer. These add tartness and sharpness to counter the sweetness of your ice cream, and also give another dash of fruit into the equation. You could also use witbier for a slightly more savoury, spicy jelly – but for best results, look to anything containing berries...

Pop the cork of a framboise – the raspberry lambic often used as an apéritif in the Low Countries – and get ready for the most vibrant-looking beer to appear. Deep pinkish ruby with a slightly pink head, this is a confident beer right from the off. The fruit is the dominant aroma and flavour (as you would hope) but also in there is a reasonable hit of sourness from the spontaneously fermented lambic. At only 2.5% ABV, this fruit beer isn't going to floor you – it's aimed more at quick and easy enjoyment, refreshment, and being added to a jelly to be served alongside your favourite ice cream (where we're concerned).

Soak the gelatine sheets in cool water for a few minutes, until they become soft and floppy when you pick them up. In the meantime, heat the sugar with 500ml (18fl oz) of framboise – the best part of 2 bottles – until it has dissolved. You don't want to boil the beer, but adding sugar to the tart liquid will help balance the jelly, and also knock some of the carbonation out.

Add the drained gelatine sheets and continue stirring until they have dissolved. Give a squeeze of lemon over the top and decant into a series of your funkiest glassware before refrigerating for at least a couple of hours. Serve with ice cream.

SERVES 6

Ingredients:

6 sheets of gelatine
4 tablespoons caster sugar
2 bottles of Lindemans Framboise
juice of ½ lemon
ice cream, to serve

OTHER BEERS TO TRY

Timmermans Framboise Lambic,
Boon Framboise Lambic,
Drie Fonteinen Framboos

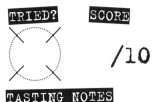

TRIED?   SCORE

/10

TASTING NOTES

STICKY TOFFEE PUDDING

Beer: BrewDog Tokyo*
Style: Imperial Stout

Sometimes you need lightness, deftness and gracefulness. And then other times you need sticky toffee pudding. To finish you off on a long winter's day – maybe after a walk through crunchy leaves or freshly fallen snow – the addition of an imperial stout to the ultimate comfort dessert makes all the more sense. Our Japanese-inspired Tokyo* is brewed with jasmine and cranberries, which give a tart bitterness to balance the sweetness of the pudding. It'll still be moreish, though – this recipe can be adapted to serve six, four, two or even just one person. It can be our little secret.

As always, start with a beer. Open a bottle of Tokyo* and pour out a sample into a small glass (you'll need 250ml/9fl oz for the recipe but you could buy two bottles and drink one as you cook, if you're making a night of it). Take in the dark fruit, chocolate and warming alcohol aromas, and then experience them again on the taste. Our intergalactic imperial stout deploys the slight tartness of cranberries to dial back the sweetness from the enormous malt bill – leaving a perfectly balanced beer (even at 16.5% ABV). Don't get carried away, though: we need the rest for the sticky toffee pudding!

Preheat the oven to 180°C/350°F/gas mark 4 and line a 20cm (8 inch) square tin with baking parchment.

Gently warm the dates and 250ml (9fl oz) of the beer in a small pan over a medium heat, until the dates become soft. Be careful not to boil the beer, as this will impair the flavour. Allow to cool and mash with a fork into a thick purée.

In a bowl, mix together the flour, bicarbonate of soda and mixed spice. Beat the eggs and vanilla in a separate bowl. In a third (large) bowl, beat the butter and caster sugar together for a few minutes until slightly creamy.

Add the beaten eggs to the butter a little at a time, beating well in between. Using a large metal spoon, gently fold in the flour, then stir in the beer-soaked dates. The mix may look a little curdled at this point and will be like a soft, thick batter. Spoon into the tin and bake for 30–35 minutes, until risen and firm.

Meanwhile, put the brown sugar, syrup and butter into a medium saucepan with half the cream. Bring to the boil over a medium heat, stirring all the time, until the sugar has completely dissolved. Turn up the heat slightly and let the mixture bubble away for 2–3 minutes, until it is a rich toffee colour, stirring occasionally to make sure it doesn't burn. Take the pan off the heat and beat in the rest of the cream.

Remove the pudding from the oven and leave to cool. Loosen it well from the sides of the tin with a small knife and turn it out. You can slice and serve it straight away with the sauce drizzled over, or refrigerate and reheat in the microwave when needed (it also freezes really well).

Whenever you serve it, the pairing with our resonant imperial stout is amazing – the sweetness of the sauce is tamed by the roasty, deep flavours of the beer, while the addition of Tokyo* to the dates brings a complementary flavour to the pudding, bridging that gap to our beer. The challenge is not to make it every week.

NB Tokyo has a long brewing period and is brewed intermittently so can be difficult to get hold of from time to time.

SERVES 6

Ingredients:

For the sponge
225g (8oz) dates, stoned
   and chopped
1 bottle of BrewDog Tokyo*
225g (8oz) self-raising flour
¾ teaspoon bicarbonate of soda
1 teaspoon mixed spice
3 eggs
1 teaspoon vanilla extract
100g (3½oz) unsalted butter
225g (8oz) golden caster sugar

For the sauce
250g (9oz) soft light brown sugar
275ml (9½fl oz) golden syrup
110g (4oz) unsalted butter
225ml (8fl oz) double cream

OTHER BEERS TO TRY

AleSmith Speedway Stout,
Mikkeller Beer Geek Brunch Weasel,
Founders Breakfast Stout

TRIED?   SCORE

       /10

TASTING NOTES

LAST
ORDERS

BREWDOG SPOTTER'S GUIDE

BREWDOG

Name: _____

Date: _____

Beers Sampled

1. _____ ☐
2. _____ ☐
3. _____ ☐
4. _____ ☐
5. _____ ☐
6. _____ ☐
7! _____ ☐
8! _____ ☐
9!! _____ ☐
10!! _____ ☐

BrewDog Bar: _____

Time in: **Time Out:**

External Weather

☐   ☐   ☐   ☐   ☐

On this visit, I was drinking with:

Friends ☐
Romans ☐
Countrymen ☐
Nobody ☐
My dog ☐
Someone else's dog ☐
Co-workers ☐
Beer geeks ☐

Would you rather be anywhere else?

Yes ☐   NO! ☐

If yes, where would you rather be and why?

_____
_____
_____
_____
_____
_____
_____
_____

While in _____ **I saw:**

Someone being ID'd ☐

Did they have any? _____
_____
_____
_____

Someone on a laptop ☐

What were they looking at? _____
_____
_____
_____

What do you think the favourite beer of the person who served you is? _____

_____

What is it really? _____

_____

Beer of the night was... _____

_____

Why? _____

_____

Bar Playlist

Metal ☐

Other _____

_____

_____

_____

DOGWATCH

Small ☐

Feisty ☐ } ☐

Medium ☐

Large ☐

Jumbo ☐

Highest number at once

_____

I imagine their names were

_____

Their names were

_____

What's the most famous thing about the city you are drinking in? _____

_____

_____

_____

What should it be? _____

_____

_____

_____

_____

I saw someone reading:

This book ☐

War & Peace ☐

Newspaper ☐

Betting coupon ☐

Other: _____

_____

_____

_____

_____

Highest beard count _____

Band T-shirt ☐
What band _____

Brewery T-shirt ☐
What brewery _____

Which was... cooler? _____

More stained? _____

Any other observations? _____

_____

_____

_____

_____

_____

_____

_____

_____

_____

BREWDOG SPOTTER'S GUIDE

BREWDOG

Name: _____

Date: _____

Beers Sampled

1. _____ ☐
2. _____ ☐
3. _____ ☐
4. _____ ☐
5. _____ ☐
6. _____ ☐
7! _____ ☐
8! _____ ☐
9!! _____ ☐
10!! _____ ☐

BrewDog Bar: _____

Time in: **Time Out:**

External Weather

☐   ☐   ☐   ☐   ☐

On this visit, I was drinking with:

Old friends ☐
New friends ☐
Boyfriend ☐
Girlfriend ☐
A stranger ☐
Teammates ☐
Soulmate ☐
Out a care ☐

Would you rather be anywhere else?

Yes ☐   **NO!** ☐

If yes, where would you rather be and why?

_____
_____
_____
_____
_____
_____
_____
_____
_____

While in _____ **I saw:**

A beer flight ordered ☐
Was it you? _____

_____

Someone taking notes in a book ☐
An unusual animal ☐
What was it? _____

A beer spilled ☐

Who knocked it over _____

What beer was it? _____

_____

Were there tears? _____

What do you think the favourite beer of the person who served you is? _____

_____

What is it really? _____

_____

Beer of the night was... _____

_____

Why? _____

_____

Bar Playlist

Country ☐

Other _____

_____

_____

_____

DOGWATCH

White ☐

Golden ☐

Brown ☐ }☐

Red ☐ **Mix**

Black ☐

Best-behaved colour?

_____

Worst-behaved colour?

_____

Did they meet?

_____

What's the best thing about the bar you are drinking in? _____

_____

_____

_____

What would make it even better?

_____

_____

_____

I saw someone reading:

This book ☐

Harry Potter ☐

Takeaway menu ☐

Someone's palm ☐

Other: _____

_____

_____

_____

_____

Any other observations? _____

_____

_____

_____

_____

_____

_____

_____

Droptick for your favourite beer this visit

TRIED & TASTED!

THIS DROPTICK WAS...

_____

AND I SCORED IT _____ /10

BREWDOG SPOTTER'S GUIDE

BREWDOG

Name: _____

Date: _____

Beers Sampled

1. _____ ☐
2. _____ ☐
3. _____ ☐
4. _____ ☐
5. _____ ☐
6. _____ ☐
7! _____ ☐
8! _____ ☐
9!! _____ ☐
10!! _____ ☐

BrewDog Bar: _____

Time in: **Time Out:**

External Weather

☐   ☐   ☐   ☐   ☐

On this visit, I was drinking with:

The boys ☐
The girls ☐
The bar staff ☐
A real punk ☐
Indiana Jones ☐
My dog(s) ☐
A whisky chaser ☐
Aplomb ☐

Would you rather be anywhere else?

Yes ☐   **NO!** ☐

If yes, where would you rather be and why?

_____
_____
_____
_____
_____
_____
_____
_____
_____
_____

What do you think the favourite beer of the person who served you is? _____

_____

What is it really? _____

_____
_____

Beer of the night was... _____

_____
_____

Why? _____

_____
_____

Bar Playlist

Speed polka ☐

Other _____

_____

_____

_____

DOGWATCH

Short hair ☐

Curly hair ☐

Wiry hair ☐

Shaggy hair ☐

No hair ☐

Hair length of quietest dog

_____

Hair length of loudest dog

_____

Number wearing cone of shame

_____

I saw someone reading:

This book ☐

50 Shades of Grey ☐

An e-book reader ☐

Horoscopes ☐

Other: _____

_____

_____

_____

_____

If your next beer could be served in another city where would it be?

_____

_____

_____

What beer would you ask for?

_____

_____

_____

While in _____ I saw:

A couple arguing ☐

What do you think it was about?_____

_____

More people on phones than talking ☐

Five people in a row ordering the same beer ☐

What was it?_____

A celebrity ☐

Who was it?_____

A celebrity look alike ☐

Who was it?_____

How close to the real person _____

Who do you wish it was?_____

_____

Any other observations? _____

_____

_____

_____

_____

_____

_____

_____

_____

_____

_____

_____

_____

_____

_____

_____

_____

_____

_____

_____

JAMES & MARTIN'S BAR CRAWL

You can't always appreciate beer in your hermetically sealed tasting chamber. Sometimes you need to get out there and experience the local stuff with the men and women who enjoy it the most. If you ever find yourself in these particular necks of the woods, make like us and head straight for these amazing bars. You can always check into your hotel later.

Stone Brewing World Bistro & Gardens

Escondido, California, USA

www.stonebrewing.com/visit/bistros/escondido

Stone's original destination taproom is a colossal bistro set in a lush garden, yet still retaining a cosy, friendly atmosphere. With 36 taps of amazing craft beer, the food menu is rife with pairing suggestions and the choice of dishes is something even non-beer drinkers would appreciate. A must-visit if you ever find yourself near San Diego.

Nidaba

Montebelluna, Italy

www.facebook.com/NidabaBeerPeaceLove

Speaking of mottoes, Nidaba's is "beer, peace and love", which oddly seems to fit well with the skull-based decor. This perfect emporium of Italian craft beer and food is located an hour north of Venice, and brings a level of innovation to both the cooking and the pairings that is seldom seen in even the highest-end restaurants. Nidaba is truly stunning.

Duke's Brew & Que

London, UK

www.dukesbrewandque.com

The barbecue joint that gave birth to Beavertown, Duke's motto of "love meat, love beer" is as simple as its heaving plates are delicious. For the best ribs in town, coupled with any one of a dozen London-brewed craft beers, Duke's is the place to head – even if you have to queue, the line will be worth it in the end.

Churchkey

Washington DC, USA

www.churchkeydc.com

The staff at Churchkey work harder than anyone to get your beer to you in the best possible way, and a total focus on quality, clean lines and temperature-controlled cellars (three of them, in fact) leave the 50 taps and five casks in perfect hands. Possibly the best place for cask-conditioned ale in the USA, Churchkey also serves amazing food and is a haven for any beer fan in the DC area (and beyond).

Bakushu Club Popeye

Tokyo, Japan

www.lares.dti.ne.jp/~ppy

Japan's pulsating capital of light has plenty of distractions for the curious traveller, and a short hop from the Edo-Tokyo Museum is another institution of learning (albeit with more atmosphere). Bakushu Club Popeye (*bakushu* is the Japanese for "beer") is one of the best bars in the world, and a perfect introduction to the incredible new variety of Japanese beer.

Chez Moeder Lambic

Brussels, Belgium

www.moederlambic.com

In a city with memorable beer on every street corner, a bar in Brussels needs to do something to stand out from the crowd. Moeder Lambic does the opposite, resting on its principle of perfectly served, constantly changing beer from Belgium and around the world. Why do anything more? Get a seat outside during the summer and keep the beers coming.

Feral Brewing Company Brewhouse

Swan Valley, Australia

www.feralbrewing.com.au

This part of the world may be wine country, but if you need to chill out with amazing beer in Western Australia then Feral is the place to head. Fantastic beers brewed on site with a truly massive veranda – which is misted with cooling spray in the heat of summer – and a brilliant restaurant as well. The food and beer pairings are not to be missed.

Tørst

Brooklyn, New York, USA

www.torstnyc.com

With no shortage of incredible drinking options in New York, one of the very best is found down an everyday-looking street in Brooklyn. Founded by Jeppe Jarnit-Bjergsø of Danish brewers Evil Twin, its beer list is the best in the city, and the bar has an incredible tasting-menu restaurant (Luksus) to the rear. Whether eating or drinking, get there early.

BrewDog Aberdeen

Aberdeen, Scotland

www.brewdog.com/bars/uk/aberdeen

Ah, come on. We couldn't compile a global guide to the best bars without a tip of the hat toward our own forerunner. Opened in 2010, our first-ever outlet gained a loyal and beer-knowledgeable crowd from day one, and is the perfect place for those members of our BrewDog crew who live in the city to unwind after a shift.

WarPigs Brewpub

Copenhagen, Denmark

www.warpigs.dk

A co-venture between Danish brewer Mikkeller and American 3 Floyds, WarPigs is a barbecue joint and 20-beer bar in one of Europe's most tourist-friendly cities. The slow-roast Texas BBQ sells out pretty quickly, so get there early if you want to eat – but either side of that feel free to stay until you've enjoyed the full range of amazing beers on offer. This will take a while, but it will also be worth it.

GLASSWARE

1.
NONIC PINT

2.
US PINT

3.
PILSNER FLUTE

4.
WEIZEN GLASS

1 NONIC PINT

Classic British pub glass; the bulge helps bar staff to stack them and you to grip them, also allows head to develop and aids its retention as the beer is drunk.

Use for: brown ales, porters, stouts, bitters, English IPAs, milds

2 US PINT

The nonic's American equivalent is also known as the "tumbler" or "shaker" pint due to its being used for mixing cocktails. Typically smaller than a British pint at 473ml (16 fl oz), compared with 568ml (20 fl oz).

Use for: US IPA, brown ales, porters, stouts

3 PILSNER FLUTE

Large, tapering, straight glass that holds the foam of a Pilsner in check and allows the colour and clarity to be observed by everyone in the bar. It's very top-heavy, though, so watch those elbows.

Use for: lagers

4 WEIZEN GLASS

This tall, bowl-cut glass allows the billowing rolls of foam from highly carbonated wheat beers to truly unleash themselves, and also captures the aromas of these global classics.

Use for: wheat beers, bunches of flowers

5. TULIP

6. SNIFTER

7. MOSELLA

8. STANGE

5 TULIP

Once restricted to Belgium, the tulip should be your go-to workhorse item of glassware. A perfect design for discovering the aromas and flavours of pretty much every beer style.

Use for: IPAs, double IPAs, stouts, all Belgian beers, anything, really.

6 SNIFTER

Often used for the swirling of brandies, snifters are smaller than tulips and have that perfect bowl shape to emphasize the aromas of rich, heavy beers during fireside beer appreciation.

Use for: imperial stout, imperial porter, barley wine, barrel-aged beers, Berliner Weisse

7 MOSELLA

Small, stemmed tulip glasses, perfect for big-hitting beers and high-rolling beer tasters. Also ideal for short, sharp, flavourful beers (or drinking occasions).

Use for: barley wine, imperial stout, beer tasting

8 STANGE

These small, thin, straight-sided glasses are icons of the beer-glass world. Used exclusively for Kölsch, they are seen in every glassware guide but rarely in the wild (outside of Cologne).

Use for: Kölsch

GLOSSARY

WHAT DOES IT ALL MEAN?
CRAFT BEER (AND HOME-BREWING), FROM A-Z

A

ABV   Alcohol By Volume: the percentage volume of alcohol per volume of beer. Measured by laboratory analysis or using a hydrometer as an approximate (the final gravity is subtracted from the original gravity and then divided by 0.0075).

Acetaldehyde   A by-product of fermentation that presents itself as an aroma of green apples.

Acid rest   Holding the mash at 35–45°C (95–113°F) to lower the pH and break down glucans that can produce a hazy beer.

Adjunct   Rice or corn used in place of traditional grains to make beer with a lighter body (or cheaper). In reality the term "adjunct" can be used to indicate anything added to the beer that isn't typically part of a recipe. So not necessarily bad, but to be treated with caution.

Alcohol   The clear, powerful constituent of beer produced by yeast acting on sugars from the malted grains. Expressed as a percentage of volume (or more rarely these days, weight) "alcohol" is a synonym for ethyl alcohol or ethanol.

Ale   Historically brewed and fermented without hops, English ale was different to "beer", which arrived from Europe in the 15th century and did contain hops. Existing in parallel for centuries, when brewers began adding hops to their ales the two terms became synonyms.

All-malt beer   A brew relying solely on the sugars yielded from malted grains – that is, without the addition of adjuncts or other sources of fermentable sugar. AKA The Good Stuff.

Alpha acid   The source of hop bitterness – a compound found in the resin glands of hop flowers. During the boil it is isomerized (converted by heat) to iso-alpha acids, yielding bitterness in the final beer.

Anaerobic   An organism metabolizing sugars without oxygen, such as bottom-fermenting lager yeast.

Astringency   The puckering dryness on the aftertaste of a beer. Often caused by long mashes, sparging for long periods or overboiling the wort, which releases tannins. In many craft beers, an astringent bitterness isn't a fault so much as something to highlight on social media.

Attenuation   The conversion of sugars into alcohol and carbon dioxide by fermentation, reducing the specific gravity of the wort. Beers that are less attenuated will contain more residual sugar and therefore be sweeter than highly attenuated, drier beers.

B

Beer   What you are hopefully holding in your hand right now. Also, the malt-led beverage that took over the world.

BJCP   Beer Judge Certification Program: formed in 1985 to promote the tasting, evaluation and perception of beer, as well as to list the style categories for judging purposes.

Black malt   Barley roasted at high temperatures in a kiln to give dark coloration and flavours of deep roast and coffee. Often used for stouts or porters.

Body   The property of a beer relating to thickness and the sensation of palate fullness. Can range from thin to full-bodied, and depends on the proteins and sugars in the final beer.

Bottle conditioning   Yeast seeded into each bottle before capping allows the beer to continue to ferment and mature in the bottle. Additional sugar is often added (primed) to act as a continuing source of food for the yeast.

Bottom fermentation   Caused by yeast cells that sink to the base of the tank after fermentation. Often they work best at lower temperatures and have higher attenuation than top-fermenting yeasts, meaning the resultant beer is crisper and has a cleaner flavour profile. As such these yeasts are also referred to as "lager yeasts".

Brew kettle   Also known as the copper. Where wort from the mash is boiled, and hops added.

Bright beer tank (BBT)   A stainless-steel vessel in which beer is retained after primary fermentation is complete and the beer is ready for packaging.

Burtonization   Treating the water for brewing with salts so as to replicate the famed water of Burton upon Trent, which made English pale ale famous.

C

CAMRA   Campaign for Real Ale: founded in 1971 as a consumer group to preserve the British tradition of cask ale and classic pubs.

Carbonation   The addition and dissolution of carbon dioxide into a beer to give a fizz. Occurs naturally during fermentation by yeast and can also be induced artificially ("force carbonation") by the injection of gas into a keg. CAMRA is very much not a fan of this.

Chill haze   Proteins joining together when a beer is refrigerated, producing particles large enough to cause visible cloudiness when it is poured. Affects the appearance of a beer, not the taste.

Cicerone®   Programme of learning relating to the serving, culture and tasting of beer. Participants can sit exams for one of four, increasingly complex, levels – Certified Beer Server®, Certified Cicerone®, Advanced Cicerone® and Master Cicerone®.

Conditioning   The maturation of a beer following the fermentation stage. The conditioning phase rounds out the flavours of a beer while preventing the formation of anything unwanted. It also allows the yeast to settle to the bottom of the tank and aids natural carbonation. Can be done at a range of temperatures.

Contract brewing   Paying someone else to produce your beer. Often done when a brewery begins life and cannot afford or justify its own kit, or by other breweries that focus on the brand and route to market.

Craft beer   Independently owned, traditionally brewed beer made with skill, love and one eye on social media.

D

Decoction   A technique for mashing grain in which part of the wort is removed, boiled and returned. This system – developed in continental Europe – raises the temperature of the mash rapidly through a series of these heating steps, resulting in beers with rich, sweet, caramel flavours.

Dextrins   Long-chain sugars that yeasts struggle to ferment. Produced by enzymes in barley, they contribute to the gravity, body and sweetness of the final beer. Lower mashing temperatures produce a higher ratio of dextrin to fermentable sugars.

Diacetyl   A powerful compound naturally produced during fermentation that if allowed to remain in the final beer manifests itself as a buttery, butterscotch aroma and flavour. It can be re-absorbed by yeast during the "diacetyl rest" stage.

DMS   Dimethyl sulphide: another off-flavour in beer, caused by a low kilning temperature of malt, a short boiling period or bacterial infection. Results in a characteristic aroma and flavour of cooked sweetcorn or tomato soup.

Dry-hopping   Addition of dried hops directly to the fermentation vessel to give greater hop aroma and flavour without increasing bitterness. A technique that has become par for the course for craft breweries.

E

EBC   European Brewery Convention: a scale for describing the colour of a beer. Similar to the SRM scale.

Enzymes   Without enzymes, there would be no beer. They convert starches of malted barley into sugars, which are later used by yeast, and are greatly affected by change in temperatures and pH.

Esters   Compounds created during fermentation that result in fruity, flowery or spicy aromas and flavours in the final beer. Classically, Belgian beers have high levels of esters.

Extract   Concentrated wort dried or converted into a syrup and marketed as an aid to entry-level home-brewers. The first step on the road to owning your own brewery.

F

Fermentation   The metabolization of sugars by yeast into ethyl alcohol and carbon dioxide. Or, how beer is born.

Final gravity   The specific gravity of a beer when fermentation is complete.

Fining   Adding various natural or artificial substances to your conditioning beer to hasten the accumulation and sinking of matter such as yeast cells and produce a clearer beer. Many craft breweries have decided not to use finings, citing differences in flavour or the desire to make vegan-friendly beers (a commonly used fining agent being the fish-derived isinglass).

First runnings   The initial wort created during the mash that is high in sugars. Typically added back into the mash (recirculation), historically it was siphoned off and used to make a strong beer, with the rest of the mash being used for a lower-strength version.

Foudres   Supersized oak barrels commonly used in wine production but also in adding intense tart, puckering flavour to lambic and other amazing sour beers.

G

Germination   The second, most important, stage of malting. Barley is allowed to sprout and left for a few days, then dried, making it easier for brewers to get to the sugars.

Grist   Another word for the malt used in brewing, once crushed during the milling process.

Gruit   Mixture of herbs used to flavour beer prior to the use of hops.

Gypsum   An ion that results in slightly acidic brewing water. Scientifically known as calcium sulphate, gypsum was a key ingredient of the Burton pale ales and is a large part of what brewers add to their water if they are "Burtonizing" it.

H

Heat exchanger   Mechanical device used to cool the wort prior to fermentation.

Hop back   Vessel used to strain the wort before it is chilled in the heat exchanger. Removes used hops and other debris.

Hops   What we worship on a daily basis.

Hot break   Boiling of the wort to cause proteins and resins to coalesce quickly.

Hydrometer   Instrument used to calculate the specific gravity of a beer. A glass cylinder, the hydrometer bobs up and down in a sample of beer before settling and allowing the gravity to be read from a scale on the side.

I

IBU   International Bitterness Units: the scale used to measure the bitterness of a beer. Assessed as the parts per million of isomerized alpha acids present, and ranging in scale from 1 to the (theoretical and oft-exceeded) limit of 100.

Infusion   The alternative to decoction, and the most commonly used form of mash. Heated water is added at a specific, single, temperature rather than in a series of increasing steps.

Irish moss   Also known as carrageen, a powdered seaweed used to clarify beer by aiding the hot break.

Isinglass   Fining agent obtained from the swim bladders of fish and used to clarify a beer during the conditioning stage, accelerating the settling out of yeast to the bottom of the vessel.

Isomerization   The change manifested on hop alpha acids during the boiling stage that produces iso-alpha acids, which are soluble and therefore remain in the beer through to the final product.

K

Kilning   The drying of barley to stop the germination phase. Different lengths of kilning time and temperature create malts of different flavours which yield differing amounts of fermentable sugars.

Krausening   Adding a small amount of partly fermented wort from another brew to the conditioning tank. This sparks secondary fermentation and aids the developing carbonation level of the beer.

L

Lacing   The delicate-looking pattern of foam that remains on your finished glass of beer.

Lager   Beers typically produced through bottom fermentation and conditioning at cooler temperatures than ales, giving a crisper, lighter beer, which for the last 30 years, has been devalued by industrial breweries.

Lautering   The process of separating the wort from the grain at the end of the mash. This straining is often performed in a separate lauter tun, where the liquid can be filtered through the grains and siphoned off. Can also be done in the mash tun.

Light-struck   Exposed to light, UV or fluorescent wavelengths. In beer, these break down the isohumulones in the hops and give a skunk-like, weedy smell.

Liquor   In brewing, not the hard stuff; liquor is the name given to water used to mash in.

M

Malt   Barley or other grains soaked in water so that they partially germinate, before being kilned to yield a harder, brittle grain full of fermentable sugars to be harnessed by the brewer.

Mash   A mix of crushed malt and hot liquor that begins the brewing process.

Maltose   Fermentable sugar contained in malt, released in the mash.

Milling   Grinding malt to crack the husk and facilitate the release of sugars during the mash. The degree of the crushing will determine how efficient the brew is, and how many grain husks remain to act as a natural filter bed during lautering.

Mouthfeel   The generic term for the non-flavour sensations experienced when drinking a beer – such as how full it is, the level of carbonation and how long the aftertaste lasts.

N

Noble hops   Four classic Central European varietals noted for their herbal aromas and flavours. They are Saaz, Tettnang, Spalt and Halltertau.

O

Original gravity   The specific gravity of a beer before fermentation occurs.

Oxidized   Having a stale, cardboard-like aroma and flavour as a result of oxygen acting on the beer.

P

pH   How acidic or alkaline a solution is, on a scale of 1–14. Beer usually hovers around 4, but the exact level is crucial for yeast health and hop extraction rates.

Phenol   Series of aroma and flavour compounds derived from the action of yeast, from the malt or from unwanted bacterial infection. Sometimes they are sought-after by the brewers (such as the clovey aromas of witbiers or the smoky flavour of Rauchbier) and sometimes they are not (the unwanted infections).

Pitching   Adding yeast to wort so that fermentation can begin.

Priming   Adding sugar to home-brewed bottles to promote secondary fermentation.

R

Real ale   What CAMRA lives for – beers that have undergone secondary fermentation in the cask (or bottle) and, in a pub, are served without the addition of extraneous gas.

Reinheitsgebot   German "Purity Law" originating in 1516 and requiring that only malted grains, hops and water be used in the brewing. Extended to include yeast when it was discovered.

S

Saccharification   The action of converting starch into fermentable sugars.

Secondary fermentation   The continuing action of yeast inside a sealed container.

Session beer   A lower-strength, lighter-bodied beer that can be enjoyed in volume on a weeknight.

Sparging   Spraying the mash with warm water to remove as many of the sugars as possible at the end of the mash. Often performed in a lauter tun.

Specific gravity   A liquid's density compared to water – essentially, the amount of sugar that is dissolved in a liquid. Pure water has a specific gravity of 1.000.

SRM (Standard Reference Method)   Adopted in 1951, an American scale to measure the colour of a beer. Runs from 2 (pale straw) to 40 (black).

T

Top fermentation   Caused by yeast cells that remain near the top of the vessel after fermentation. They traditionally work better at warmer temperatures than those that sink to the bottom and produce a beer with a richer, sweeter, fruitier flavour. As such, these yeasts are referred to as "ale yeasts".

Trub   Particles left in the bottom of a vessel – the result of allowing a developing beer to rest and have anything in suspension sink to the bottom to be removed. Can be dead yeast, precipitate proteins, hop debris. Nothing tasty.

V

Volatiles   Compounds that evaporate when exposed to air or when in a liquid that is boiled. Some hop oils are notoriously volatile and can be lost during the boil. The volatility of many off-flavour compounds also means that they can be deliberately removed by boiling.

Vorlauf   The recirculation of the first runnings of wort – as well as being full of sugars, the initial liquid run-off from the mash will be cloudy and full of particulates, so it is often collected and poured back on top of the grain bed to run through a second time. The process is named after the German word for "temporary".

W

Whirlpool   A vessel that collects the particulate matter following lautering, spinning the wort so that the debris settles in the centre and the liquid can be siphoned from the sides.

Wort   The proto-beer solution strained from the mash tun. Full of sugars, it is the liquid that yeasts act on to convert it into beer.

Z

Zymurgy   The study of yeast and fermentation

FURTHER READING

As much as you enjoy tasting, evaluating and talking about beer, there is nothing like sitting back with a good book (as you are hopefully realizing now). Here is a short reading list of volumes to help further, broaden and increase your beery knowledge.

Business for Punks – James Watt (*Portfolio Penguin, 2015*)

Amber, Gold and Black – Martyn Cornell (*The History Press, 2010*)

The Audacity of Hops – Tom Acitelli (*Chicago Review Press, 2013*)

Beer and Food – Mark Dredge (*Dog and Bone, 2014*)

Beer, Food and Flavour – Schuyler Schultz (*Skyhorse Publishing, 2012*)

Beer: The Story of the Pint – Martyn Cornell (*Headline, 2003*)

Brew Britannia – Jessica Boak & Ray Bailey (*Aurum Press, 2014*)

Brew Like a Monk – Stan Hieronymus (*Brewers' Publications, 2005*)

Brewed Awakening – Joshua M. Bernstein (*Sterling Epicure, 2011*)

The Brewmaster's Table – Garrett Oliver (*HarperCollins, 2003*)

Craft Beer World – Mark Dredge (*Dog and Bone, 2013*)

The Craft of Stone Brewing Co.
   – Greg Koch, Steve Wagner, Randy Clemens (*Ten Speed Press, 2011*)

Designing Great Beers – Ray Daniels (*Brewers' Publications, 1996*)

Man Walks into a Pub – Pete Brown (*MacMillan, 2003*)

Mikkeller Book of Beer
   – Mikkel Borg Bjergsø and Pernille Pang (*Jacqui Small, 2014*)

IPA – Mitch Steele (*Brewers' Publications, 2012*)

The Oxford Companion to Beer
   – Garrett Oliver, Editor (*Oxford Press, 2011*)

Tasting Beer – Randy Mosher (*Storey Publishing, 2009*)

Wood & Beer: A Brewers' Guide
   – Dick Cantwell & Peter Brouckaert (*Brewers' Publications, 2016*)

ACKNOWLEDGEMENTS

Time to raise a glass to everyone who took the time to help in the production of this book. The beer drinkers of the world thank you!

Karl Adamson, Pauline Bache, Ron Barchet, Shaun Barnes, Denise Bates, David Beattie, Frank Boon, Oliver Boulton, Sam Brill, Alex Buchanan, Richard Burhouse, Stefan Butz, Linda Campbell, Jonathan Christie, Ben Clark, Martyn Cornell, Ray Daniels, Gaëlle Denies, Olivier Dedeycker, Tiago Falcone, Allan Grant, Kamilla Hannibal, Jody Hartley, Sian Henley, Dave Higgins, Franz Horak, Tony Hutchinson, Suzanne Irvine, Tami Jermyn, Denis Johnstone, Paul Jones, Scott Kolbe, Mark Krawiec, Mark Lambert, Rob Lovatt, Rob Mackay, Alison McDonald, Craig Middleton, Alan Mochrie, Johnny Moran, Gemma Oliviero, Pernille Pang, Manu Pauwels, Claire Phillips, Geoff Quinn, Dan Reed, Stuart Ross, Matt Shaw, Simon Shaw, Allan Stone, Jack Storey, Colin Stronge, Paula Taylor, Matthias Trum, Guillaume Vandooren, Al Wall, Paul Winch-Furness, Allan Wright, Lloyd Wright, Lizzie Younkin.

INDEX

UK/US GLOSSARY

UK   US

Adverts   Advertisements

Autumn   Fall

Beef mince   Ground beef

Bespoke   Customized

Bicarbonate of soda   Baking soda

Biscuit   Cookie

Blitz   Process, blend

Bramley apple   Can use another
cooking apple, such as Granny Smith

Cake tin   Cake pan

Caster sugar   Superfine sugar

Chestnut mushroom   Cremini
mushroom

Chips   Fries

Chocolate fondant   Chocolate lava
cake

Coriander leaves   Cilantro

Cornflour   Cornstarch

Crisps   Potato chips

Crumble   Crisp, when referring
to a dessert

Curry   Can refer to having an Indian
meal, similar to a reference to having
a Mexican or Chinese meal

Dark chocolate   Semisweet
chocolate; if 62% cocoa or more,
use bittersweet chocolate

Double cream   Heavy cream

Expiry date   Expiration date

Golden syrup   Use light corn syrup

Griddled   Grilled

Grill   Broil or broiler when in the oven;
grill on the stove or a barbecue

Groundnut oil   Peanut oil

Haggis   A type of Scottish sausage
made with oats and variety meats

Headmaster   School principal

Icing sugar   Confectioners' sugar,
also known as powdered sugar

Jelly   Gelatin

Kitchen paper   Paper towels

Knob of butter   Pat of butter

Leaves of gelatine   Gelatin sheets

Maize   Corn

Mash (with sausages)   Mashed
potatoes

Measuring jug   Liquid measuring cup

Mixed spice   Blend of spices similar
to allspice

Moreish   Creating a desire for more

Mushy peas   Traditional British way
of preparing peas to be served with
fish or pies; serve these with normal
peas instead

Muslin   Cheesecloth

Nanny state   Refers to an
overprotective government, acting
like a nanny protecting a child

Noughties   2000s

Palm sugar   Can substitute with
brown sugar

Passata   Tomato puree or sauce

Pavement   Sidewalk

Pub/public house   Licensed bar

Plain white flour   All-purpose flour

Ploughman's   Cold lunch with bread,
cheese and pickle

Pork scratching   Pork crackling/rind

Prawns   Shrimp

Rocket   Arugula

Scales   Kitchen scale

Scheme   Plan, program

Self-raising flour   Substitute with
all-purpose flour but for each
125g/4oz/1 cup, add 1 teaspoon
baking powder

Semi-skimmed milk   Low-fat milk

Sieve   Sift

Spring onion   Scallion

Sticky toffee pudding   Moist sponge
cake with a butterscotch-like toffee
sauce

Sweetcorn (tin of)   Corn kernels
(can of)

Tagine   Middle Eastern stew

Tesco   Large UK grocery store chain

Tick   Checkmark (adj.) or check
(noun)

Tomato purée   Tomato paste

Treacle   Similar to molasses

Trolley   Shopping cart

Vanilla pod   Vanilla bean

PICTURE CREDITS

CRAFT B
CRAFT B
FT BEER
FT BEER
CRAFT B
CRAFT B
FT BEER